<u>Praise for *Living a Life of Gratitude*</u>

"Sara taps into the music of the spheres and offers it to us in short, simple stories filled with high-energy and a purity of spirit that makes the soul sing…Highly recommended!"

—Debra Moffitt, author of *Garden of Bliss*

"Every minute of our lives is a gift, even on the days that this seems hard to remember. Each of these 88 gratitude stories helps us recall what it means to be fully present in the world."

—Margaret Ann Lembo, author of *Chakra Awakening*

"This book is a daily dose of healing medicine for your soul. Sharing personal stories and insights from her own life, stories that will melt the crust of worry from your heart and open you to the Divine, Sara Wiseman provides comforting guidance and wisdom. With tales of daily life, of relationship, of delightful everyday miracles, she offers you a glimpse into your own heart, opportunities for the growth of your own soul that come from a life lived with gratitude. I'm grateful she created this lovely book!"

—Jane Peterson, PhD, Executive Director of The Human Systems Institute

"Gratitude is a way of being—a way of living and looking at the world. Sara Wiseman shows us this over and over again, in these 88 warm, funny, richly textured stories. Heart-opening, inspiring and often moving, this book will wake you up and remind you of the true blessings of your life."

—Rita Mills, Publisher of *The New Era Times*

Living a Life of
Gratitude

About the Author

Spiritual teacher and intuitive Sara Wiseman (Oregon) is the author of *Writing the Divine: How to Use Channeling for Soul Growth & Healing*, *Your Psychic Child: How to Raise Intuitive & Spiritually Gifted Kids of All Ages*, and *Becoming Your Best Self: The Guide to Clarity, Inspiration and Joy*, all published with Llewellyn.

A branding expert for decades, she writes the "Trending Now" column for *Retailing Insight* (formerly *New Age Retailer*) and is a regular contributor to *DailyOm*. Previously a top national copywriter and features journalist, her articles on wellness, lifestyle, spirituality, and psychic development have appeared in numerous publications across the country, as well as online.

Wiseman is also an award-winning singer/songwriter for the band Martyrs of Sound, and hosts the call-in radio show "Ask Sara" on *Contact Talk Radio*. She offers private intuitive consults and training, and has worked with thousands of clients worldwide.

You can visit her website at www.sarawiseman.com.

Living a Life of Gratitude

Your Journey to Grace, Joy & Healing

Sara Wiseman

Llewellyn Publications
Woodbury, Minnesota

FIRST EDITION
First Printing, 2013

Book design by Bob Gaul
Cover design by Lisa Novak
Cover art: Background © iStockphoto.com/Oksana Pasishnychenko
Part page art: Background © iStockphoto.com/Oksana Pasishnychenko

Llewellyn Publications is a registered trademark of Llewellyn Worldwide Ltd.

Library of Congress Cataloging-in-Publication Data (Pending)
978-0-7387-37539

Llewellyn Worldwide Ltd. does not participate in, endorse, or have any authority or responsibility concerning private business transactions between our authors and the public.

All mail addressed to the author is forwarded but the publisher cannot, unless specifically instructed by the author, give out an address or phone number.

Any Internet references contained in this work are current at publication time, but the publisher cannot guarantee that a specific location will continue to be maintained. Please refer to the publisher's website for links to authors' websites and other sources.

Llewellyn Publications
A Division of Llewellyn Worldwide Ltd.
2143 Wooddale Drive
Woodbury, MN 55125-2989
www.llewellyn.com

Printed in the United States of America

Dedication

If you already know how to live with a grateful heart, this book honors you. If you are in the process of learning how to live this way, well … this book is wholly and completely dedicated to you, and to all of us who accompany you on the journey.

Acknowledgements

I am grateful to the beautiful souls who showed up as miracles during the writing of this book: the listeners of my radio show who sent their love from all over the world; the many folks who emailed me with their experiences and kind words; the very perceptive folks at Llewellyn; Dr. Steve Koc; and my children.

Contents

Part Three: Connection

Part Four: Love

Part Seven: Nature

Part Eight: Awareness

Part Nine: Awakening

Part Ten: Presence

Part Eleven: Transition

Part Twelve: Birth

Introduction

In the moment we give thanks, everything changes.

Our hearts crack open. We are flooded with love and light. And in that exact instant, we shift from our negative state to an awareness that is positive, joyous and brimming with bliss—we experience the Divine healing that is our birthright.

The trick is to learn how to create this moment not just once in our lifetimes, but over and over again.

The secret is found in gratitude—in the surrender to the grateful heart, the open heart, the heart that willingly walks in the magic and the mystery—not just for a moment or moments, but at all times.

In essence, to become grateful is to become Divine. It's a life's journey, walked step by step, on the path that unfolds before us.

Now, it all sounds fantastic, wonderful, amazing—except that at first, most of us aren't very good at being grateful. We're rusty. We're resistant. We've forgotten how to live in wonder and awe. Even as we commit to a gratitude practice, we get off track, we backslide, we slip into our habits of negativity and blame … and oh yes, we struggle!

Most of us would agree that it's not always easy to choose gratitude. Yet with perseverance, gently coming back to this place of thanks over and over again, something begins to change inside us, and we begin to move toward the light, like a flower turning to the sun.

And as we continue and simply keep going—whether it takes us days or weeks or months or years—our practice becomes second nature, until a kind of tipping point is reached, and we begin to live in this state of appreciation not just daily, but hourly, even minute to minute.

In other words, we begin to experience gratitude as our present reality.

This is possible for anyone, no matter what the starting point. For when we slow down enough to really become present in our lives—even if it's just for a few minutes a day—gratitude begins to open in our hearts. At first it's a tiny sliver, and then a cascade of healing light, until we can literally feel the energy pouring into our lives, infusing and illuminating everything that we know and that we do not know.

My journey to gratitude

My own journey to gratitude has been a life's progression, but was punctuated by a near death experience in 2008, during which I experienced a sudden and unexpected spiritual awakening accompanied by psychic opening. Since that time, I've shared my understanding and teachings with tens of thousands of people via my books, radio shows, and consults.

During the year that I wrote this book, my journey to gratitude was expanded yet again, when I had a second brush with death due to cancer. Thankfully, I am a survivor, but this experience shook me to the core, stripped away old beliefs and attachments, and ultimately deepened my spiritual understanding to a level that I would never have arrived at on my own.

So many of us have suffered in these ways: the trauma of grave or difficult experiences that lead us to greater understanding and opening of the heart. These challenges are not easy to deal with, but the rewards are many, if you choose to perceive them this way.

While I didn't expect to be experiencing my own mortality while writing this book, the reality nonetheless arrived, and it has informed this writing a thousand fold, as I learned how to open my heart again, once more into gratitude for simply what is.

It is my hope that these stories will also inform and be useful to you.

How to use this book

You can use this book as a daily teaching in your own gratitude practice, or as a source of guidance to use whenever you need it simply by turning to a story at random. You may certainly trust that the Universe will guide you to the exact page you need!

If you're using this book as a daily practice, I invite you to be gentle with yourself in your determination. For example, if you forget a day, or even a week or month, don't worry. Simply come back to the practice when you are ready. It will be still be waiting for you! Come back when you feel the pull until the secret of gratitude has unlocked in your heart and you can't imagine any other way to live.

As you journey through this book, I also invite you to connect energetically to the people and situations you'll read about, inspired by my own life and the experiences of those I've connected with in my work. Close your eyes from time to time as you read, and consider all of these souls together, our collective soul gathered in the sharing of the experiences in this book.

The questions at the end of each story are both simple and deep. Use them to help you go deeper and to make emotional connections to what is truly important in your own life.

Finally, for those who enjoy listening to audio, you will find many of these stories in audio book form at www.sarawiseman.com.

In gratitude, let us begin.

Part One:
Birth

....

*In which we enter the world
as new souls on earth.*

1

There is only one entrance

Birth is the only way we enter this world, and death is our only exit.

We all share this truth of human existence—and yet our births and deaths are as individual and unique as each of us.

Imagine!

A new soul, entering the world from the vessel of another body! A new soul, arriving by Divine choice and by Divine selection of a particular mother, a particular father.

The miracle of welcoming a new soul affects us so deeply, it's almost impossible to express everything we hold in our heart. Sit down with a group of mothers of any age or stage of childrearing, and the stories will come tumbling out…

"My first child struggled and was delivered by Caesarean. She spent three days in intensive care."

"My baby was delivered in two hours, it was the easiest, most beautiful thing I'd ever known."

"We delivered our youngest on the side of the highway, while racing to the hospital."

"My fifth child came on a full moon, on the eve of summer solstice."

"My child arrived with a full head of black hair, which he has kept to this day."

Each birth, so breathtakingly unique. The baby is born. The baby is cleansed. The baby is swaddled and returned to the mother, and the moment is overwhelmingly beautiful.

This is how we humans enter the world, and it is a miracle.

Most of us don't remember the moment of our birth—the seconds in which we were pulled from our mother's warm, sustaining womb into a new life.

Of course, some of us do—in my work as a spiritual teacher and intuitive counselor, I often guide people in past life regressions. Doing this work, I've come across a few folks who do indeed recall their gestation, their birth, the weeks and months after birth when they were very new to the world. These people recall holding the very stars in their eyes until those memories gently fade, and by age four or five they have replaced the dazzling energy of the Universe with the more gritty reality of life on earth.

Yet most of us remember nothing of our births, of these early years. We don't remember the Universe reflected in our eyes. We don't recall the mystery. Many of us don't even awaken to the miracle of our own humanity until the ages of thirteen, twenty-six, forty-nine, seventy-eight.

When any child is born, however, there is a universal knowing that this is a miracle. We understand with deep recognition that there is now a new soul on earth, and that this innocent new being will surely live, love, struggle, learn, and embark on life's path with his or her destiny already partly foretold by the time and place in which he or she is born.

Will he succeed? Will she fail? Will he find love? Will she marry? Will he have life's passion? Will she have a life's purpose?

Will he or she find the Divine as a guiding post, so that their hearts may be opened fully, and that each moment may appear as miraculous as the moment of their birth, in which they are born, cleansed, swaddled?

We don't know.

Life is a mystery.

At the moment of a new soul's birth, a new entry into this world, we see this clearly: how little we know, how much is mystery—how much is sheer wonder. And at this moment, we revisit again the progression of our own lives, and the miracle it is to have a lifetime at all.

————

Close your eyes, and allow yourself to drift into a memory of when you were born, a new soul to the world. You may recall the blanket you had, the room you slept in, a toy. You may be surprised how much you remember! Think about your birth, and give thanks that you were born, to experience this lifetime.

2

Mother is the first Beloved

Years ago, I worked with a gifted hypnotherapist. He was a newbie to the craft, just starting out, and I don't think either he or I understood the scope of his abilities then.

Suffice it to say I went to places and spaces that were far beyond the price of his introductory sessions!

We worked together in the dank basement room of a rental office downtown, the kind of place where folks set up flimsy folding tables and phone banks, then clear out overnight to whereabouts unknown. It was a way-stop for fly-by-night businesses, filled with all the ghosts of failed dreams, hush and hurry, people in unrest.

My own sessions, however, were deeply productive. I leaned back in a faux leather lounger, closed my eyes, and was transported to amazing places: I saw the Book of Knowledge, a large tome up on a larger table, in which I might turn each page and find yet another picture from my own life, a picture I might look at, and go deeper still. I found the long path of trees, a winding boulevard of sorts, that we are all somehow destined to walk. And during these sessions I also descended in, entered deeper, and ended up in a room I had forgotten for a very long time: the living room of the house I lived in when I was perhaps one or two or three.

I found myself very young—my head did not reach the countertop—in a small, hot kitchen with the radio on, and my mother, visibly pregnant, dancing. We were listening to the radio, the three of us—my mother, me, and my unborn brother in her belly. We danced to the songs of the times, the radio wailing tinny and small.

Everything in the room rushed forth all at once: the speckled, reflective bits of metallic in the kitchen counter top, the thickness of the mug in the sink, the green bottle of Palmolive on the counter, the window opening on to a back hedge, glossy with broad green leaves. My hands were slightly sticky, as if I'd just eaten lunch.

My mother wore capri pants; the kind that were popular back then, in a bold shade of sea green. In my regression, I saw clearly the way her pants ended in the middle of her calf, and I had the overwhelming thought: *she was so very young.*

And in my session, I began to cry.

She was so very young.

Not yet 30, on this ordinary day in which she danced to the radio, alone in a small kitchen, finishing the dishes from lunch, no one there save her tiny daughter and unborn son.

Mother is the first Beloved. Whether this is good or bad, it is your soul's agreement upon entering the world. We choose our parents, for reasons that may be unclear to us in this reality, but that our soul understands and accepts as an absolute necessity for growth and expansion in this lifetime.

Mother is the first Beloved, the earth soul that answers the new soul, or the new soul that answers the earth soul, and it is not always clear which soul is calling which. The child chooses the parent certainly; but on a soul level, the parent must also welcome, or at the very least allow, the child.

Sometimes both souls long for each other with ineffable longing, and it is a mutual calling between mother and child.

Your own mother held you in her womb for nine months; you were created of her body, you ate of her body, you drank of her like some divine feminine version of holy communion. You were sustained by her womb, her breath, her physical self. In this way you were entered into the world.

Sometimes moving in Divine energy of trance and regression reveals something you need to remember about your first Beloved: in this case, it was the hem of the sea green capris that helped me understand how young my mother really was when she raised me, how new as a mother, how undeveloped as a person, how young to have moved away from family to the West Coast. I saw for the first time how she might have felt spending her days alone in a tiny house, filled with hope and fierceness for her new life and her children.

Mother is the first Beloved; we have known her many times before in the karmic passage of previous lifetimes, and we will know her many times again. She is the person who makes it possible for us to enter the world, whether she is fully evolved or only beginning her journey to consciousness, whether she wanted to welcome us or not.

The first Beloved gazes at us, holds us to her breast. The first Beloved allows us to live in and of her body. The first Beloved is most times no wise, ascended saint or master—just a young woman, unsure and unguided, doing her best to bring a new soul into the world.

———

Close your eyes, and breathe deeply. Go to a place in your mind or your memory in which you can recall something about your own mother, your first Beloved, when you were very, very young. It may be a special blanket, the way the light falls in a forgotten room, a texture, a color, a smell. Go into this place, and feel everything. Because you were so young, your memory will be two ways: that of a young soul, and that of a soul who has not yet forgotten how to hold the stars in your eyes. Remember it all, and allow yourself to feel gratitude. Learn something new from this exercise about your mother, and hold it in your heart.

3
Father is the first teacher

My bathing cap is too tight; it doesn't hold the cascade of hair that someone's piled on my head in order to squash it on, pull it tight until it covers my ears. When I take it off later, my hair will be sodden, snarled, and the long strands will catch in the cap, causing me to yelp in pain.

I wear it because I want to pretend I am immune from the water: that even when I am submerged, my body will be safe from all that scary wetness.

If we wore goggles back then, I'd have put them on, too. But goggles haven't been invented yet—at least not for child swimmers like me. I squint my eyes tightly against the sun, against the stinging chlorine, against the very large dollop of zinc oxide that has been applied to my nose in precaution against sunburn, and allow myself to descend into the whorling wet that awaits.

It's summer, I'm at the pool, I'm maybe 4 or 5, and I'm learning to swim.

It's not an easy surrender.

I gasp, my heart pounds, and I catch sign of myself in reflection: I'm a green-capped alien, the water is dangerously blue, every ripple like a flash of light along the pool's floor, and I'm hang on to the only safety I know: my father's arms, my father's chest, my father's neck, everything sturdy and comforting, covered with blond curling hair.

If he lets go, I'm sure I'll die.

If I let go, I'm sure I'll drown.

I'm learning to swim, he thinks. I'm trying to survive, I'm sure.

My body is rigid with panic, my arms clamped tight around him, and yet we don't stop. We go deeper: past my knees, past my waist, until I'm up to my neck in water.

And even as we submerge deeper, I hear his voice in my ear: relax, you're doing fine, it's okay to let go.

Relax.

You're doing fine.

It's okay to let go.

I realize now, many decades later and twelve years after his passing, that these were the only real lessons I ever needed to learn from him.

The father is also a part of the soul circle; of our primary circle. Many souls are lucky to know our fathers well and long; in this loving relationship, our fathers bestow upon us a trust in the world that cannot be taken away. When our father is here, when our father is in the house, all is right with the world.

Others recall different teachings from their fathers. There may be grave difficulties in the relationship: karmic wounds that are beyond forgiving. Still others don't know of their fathers, or their fathers flit in and out of their lives, undependable at best, heartbreaking at worst.

Sinking back into those long time ago memories, I can see other fathers at the pool now, encouraging, berating, training, teaching, ignoring, punishing, present, authentic, cruel, real, loving, gentle. All those fathers, teaching lessons.

My own father took me continually to deeper depths, letting go of me even as I held on.

Relax.

You're doing fine.

It's okay to let go.

These are the soul lessons I've been working on, lately, with nary a swim cap in sight, feet fully on dry land. You, as daughters and sons of other fathers, will have your own lessons to learn.

We all receive what we need, even on a summer day in the pool.

———

What have you learned, in accepting or rejecting your own father's teachings? The male energy moves in all of us, whether we are male or female. It is a part of us, just as everything is a part of us. Take a moment now, and be grateful for what you've learned—the lessons your father taught you, and also those lessons he failed to teach. Allow yourself to open your heart to all of it.

4

Noticing the particulate

At some point you stood there, in the first living room you ever knew, when you were new to the world, and life seemed simple. And you saw it all with new eyes: The old sofa. The worn table. Toys scattered on the floor A big picture window to let the light in.

And at some point, you were playing in this room: maybe it was Saturday and your father napped on the sofa. Maybe it was a weekday, and your mother was in the kitchen. Maybe you were happy; maybe you were sad; maybe you'd been jumping on that old sofa, or making a fort out of the couch pillows.

You were simply being yourself in your body.

And then, in that moment, something shifted.

Perhaps you caught a glimpse of a spirit from the window's corner, or perhaps something flashed in your eyes, a ray of sunlight glinting in a way you'd never seen before.

You were so young then: 2, 3, maybe 4.

Everything was still wonderment, but already, you'd started to know pain. Everything was still wonderment, but already, you'd begun to forget.

The stars in your eyes had not completely faded, but they'd become shrouded, so the dazzling deep knowing of the Universe faded to a kind of vision you'd forgotten how to use, a type of seeing that was not useful for earth life.

And yet, with this particular flash of light, it all came back to you: the sun streaming in and illuminating clouds of dust in the air, so that everything in your view were specs and glints and orbs of light, particulate upon particulate, a light-filled energy field.

And you understood once again what you had nearly forgotten, that this is what we are: particulate light, floating in constellations, floating in universes, mixed and melding, always light. This is energy, this is love, this is Divine, this is us. You knew it before you were born. You remembered it again when you were young.

You can remember it today.

As you begin to see this stuff of the Universe with your adult eyes, the visible manifestation of what we call Divine, it is easy to recall more fully who you really are, what we really are: energy, light, love.

It's all around you, it is you—not just what is seen, but what is also unseen: the energy within the energy, the space within the space, the universes within the Universe.

Begin to notice the particulate today, even if at first you only glimpse it as physical phenomenon. Today, go to a place where light is streaming. Watch the particulate dance in this stream. See it, wonder at it, wish upon it! It is not just dust mixed with light; it is the essence of everything, as are you. Look in wonder. Give thanks for what you once knew and what you are beginning to remember again.

5
Becoming the I am

When we first arrive into the world, we're so blissed out with Oneness, it's hard to track on anything else. Everything we encounter in those first weeks and months, is all part of One: Mother. Father. Toes. *Fingers.*

In wonderment we experience everything as the *Universe of us*, and we're in awe. Our toes are a source of amazement: see how they wiggle! All we have to do is think "wiggle" and our toes oblige. Our fingers move, clasp, reach and grasp! All we have to do is desire something, and our fingers grab it!

As we grow older, into toddlerhood and childhood, our body becomes our Universe—our running, stretching, jumping, dancing body—and it's utter fascination. The sheer joy of moving our bodies fills our waking hours—simply being takes our attention.

We are perfect Oneness, for those days, weeks, months, and years, until one moment, we experience something that does not feel like One.

The world cleaves asunder: we feel pain. We know discomfort. We experience anxiety. Fear takes over, and in that instant we become unbearably separate.

It's not just us and our body anymore, living in blissed being. It's us, our body, and these new and terrible things called fear, panic, anxiety.

It's the black hole, and at some point in our life—most often when we are very young—we fall down it fast and hard.

Yet interestingly, it's in this pain, in this myth of separation where we have our first consciousness of being unique. For the first time, standing alone in our crib crying for the person who does not come, or does not come soon enough, we understand that we aren't just one of One; that there's more to it.

At this time, the self begins to emerge. For the first time, we see ourselves as separate, and we begin to ask questions such as:

Who am I? How am I different? How am I unique?

Many decades later, we will visit our self again at other stages of emergence with new questions:

Why am I here? What is my life's path? What is my life's purpose?

Sigh. It's a long road of discovery, and in the end, when we reach our final stop at the end of our lifetime or when we become enlightened—whichever comes first—we see clearly: all of our questions were misguided. Separation is a myth.

And when we are emerging as our young, separate selves—this is our hero's path to walk this journey. It's our rite of passage, as we're emerging from childhood into adolescence, to have thoughts such as:

I'm different. I'm unique. I'm special.

Before we can become adult, before we can become conscious, the self which knows itself as separate must emerge.

We will develop our different, unique and special gifts—or we will neglect them. There are many ways to make this journey.

Our path begins with the first step, but we often have no idea where we're going until we've traveled for a while.

At first we are One. Then the separate self emerges. The journey back to One, whether it takes a few years, decades or a lifetime, is our journey of soul growth.

––––––––

Consider today your separate self. This is the part of you that makes you unique, special, different—even while you are also One. Think back to your childhood: what were you good at? What were your gifts and talents, the abilities that came easily to you?

Now, consider your unique, special and singular gifts and talents, whether you have used them in this lifetime yet or not. Give thanks for this separate and original self that is you.

6

The beauty of your true self shines

"Mom, I want to be beautiful," my daughter said to me one morning from the back seat as we drove to school. She was about five at the time, maybe six.

"You're beautiful already!" I answered, glancing back in the rear-view mirror to see her big eyes, her fresh, round cheeks.

"No, I want to be *really* beautiful," she insisted.

I thought for a moment.

"What kind of beauty do you want?"

"I want the kind that glows."

I looked at her in the mirror again, but the fresh, round cheeks were tilted away.

"You know, like the kind Naomi has," her little voice piped again, precise, clear, wanting to be heard.

I shifted in the driver's seat, letting the traffic swoop and flow around me. I pictured Naomi, my daughter's daycare teacher, in my mind. I saw this young teacher stepping forward to greet the kids the way she did every morning, her arms open in the welcome of a morning hug, her big smile stretching across her face.

"The way Naomi looks," my daughter repeated. "Like a love look."

I felt my hands lighten on the wheel, and suddenly I saw Naomi the way my daughter did: the way she laughed in delight when the kids came into school in the morning, how she leaned down and opened her arms to each and every one, a woman so filled with love it emanated from her body, so that every time she moved, walked into a room, turned, something luminous and light streamed out.

Naomi was lit from within.

"Naomi glows," I said aloud to the back seat with conviction, suddenly getting what my daughter had seen all along.

In the back seat, all soft cheeks and long lashes, my daughter nodded, her head bobbing up and down.

———

Who do you know that glows? Close your eyes for a moment, and bring that person into your mind. Now, feel the heart opening and gratitude that you feel when you're in the presence of such a person. While you're in this space, also recall the times when you've been that person—the person who glows. Thank yourself for this, as well.

Part Two:
Emergence

....

In which we begin to know the person we will be in this lifetime.

7

What is your calling?

When we arrive into this world, we already know our calling.

When I was eight, I wanted to be a saint.

Not for the cloister, not for the reverence. Certainly not for prostrations, mean cells, self-flagellation, or any of the other methods saints in the middle centuries used to open their consciousness.

Nor was I interested in sainthood for the creation of miracles: the welling of springs wherever I walked or the spontaneous healings of masses who followed behind me.

No.

I wanted to be a saint because I wanted the pure understanding of God.

However, since the job openings for saints were pretty rare at the time, I went on to other things. I holed up in my room: reading, writing, working on the vast array of journals, typewriters, and tape recorders that seemed to fill my bedroom of their own accord. Even from the earliest days, I was obsessed with *getting it down*—with putting my thoughts on paper, on tape, on record in the clearest way I could.

It's all gone now—like a prayer on the wind.

The technology I used back then no longer exists, or at least, I don't have it anymore. The tape recorder, the Dictaphone, the manual typewriter. The copious journals kept daily from third grade are now gone.

And thus, instead of being solely recorded, the thoughts have seeped into my bones, from the time I was a child.

The Divine did not call me once, but a million times, a billion— until I finally answered. When I consider every single job I had and every single skill I learned, it has all brought me incrementally to exactly where I am today, so that I have capacity and ability to do the tasks that are my life's calling.

It was all set up from the beginning. Every single part of it.

My calling as a writer, a teacher, is my unique path. It is no better or worse than any one else's path. It is my job description, my life's purpose, what I'm here to do.

You're here for your calling, and you have been destined for this path since you were born. Every step of your life, every lesson and skill you have learned, has been created so that you may move forward in this exact moment.

Trust this.

———

If you don't know your life's calling, close your eyes. Think back to how you spent your time when you were 8, 10, 12. What did you love, without reason? What did you aspire to then? Now, allow yourself to relax in the certainty that you are perfectly on your path, moving easily toward the clear understanding of your purpose. Give thanks to your inner awareness for helping you see what you already know.

8

Who am I?

Anika was the most physically coordinated girl I'd ever met. She showed up sinewy and strong and fearless to the first day of kindergarten, and spent first recess doing things on the monkey bars I hadn't even imagined.

I was soft, timid, unsure. Standing in the hot sun with a line of other girls behind me, the best I could do was pull my leg clumsily over the bar, and slowly roll in an awkward half circle. Beside me on the other bar, Anika whipped 'round and 'round like a performer in Cirque du Soleil as the kids cheered her on.

I loved her immediately: her missing two front teeth, the short chopped haircut that somehow proclaimed her Dutch heritage. My own hair was still long and continually snarled, requiring my mother to brush it out every morning.

Anika and I became friends. Not best friends, but neighborhood friends. When she came over after school, which she did often, she gazed past all the books and paper and pens in my room as if she didn't even see them.

She wanted to ride bikes.

"You rode your bike over here?" I asked with surprise. I was only allowed to ride my bike in the alley behind our house; never on the street.

"Sure," she said, and did a kind of stretch with her arms that showed off all her double-jointedness. "I ride my bike everywhere."

We rode the alley a few times, until Anika got bored.

"Let's do the hill," she shouted, and I gulped. I'd only done the hill one time before, with my dad standing at the bottom watching out for cars. I turned to answer, but Anika was already sailing down the alley.

She did the hill about twenty times that afternoon, while I waited at the bottom and watched for cars. She flew down, choppy bob in perfect order, going faster and faster each time. And then, to my envy, she'd pedal right back up, legs pumping, effortless.

"Here I go!" she'd holler.

"Bombs away!"

"Watch this one!"

And then suddenly

"No hands!"

And before I could scream to her all the cautionary fears: *you'll get hurt, you'll fall, that's too dangerous!*—Anika was in motion, arms clasped across her chest, rocket fast, jubilant, sailing down the hill.

"No hands!" she proclaimed again when she reached bottom, untouched and unfazed and perfectly safe.

Some of us are born to fly. Others are born to sit at the bottom and watch.

And yet...

After Anika went home, I went to my room. There were my dolls and books and paper and pens, all neatly arranged, ready to use. My own private sanctuary, where I could retreat, think, wonder, contemplate, create...

Anika could ride the hill. Yes. But in the privacy of my room, surrounded by the early tools of my craft, I was learning how to fly, too.

We don't become ourselves by doing what others do. We become ourselves in those moments in which we experience deep flow, true passion in our work. We discover our unique selves in the moments we find deep joy.

We know this early in life, but often we forget to remember.

———

What did you love to do, long ago? When was the last time you did this? When you think of how you are different, unique, special from everyone else, what are you especially grateful for? What parts of you let you fly?

9

Be your own platypus

A study[1] was done of the platypus, the venomous, egg-laying duck-billed, web-footed, beaver-tailed mammal which lives in Australia.

The study set out to determine the genome of the animal, or the entirely of the animal's hereditary information. Where did it come from? What was it made of? How did this particular animal contain so many parts of different species: reptile, bird, mammal?

The results of the study, an exhaustive sequencing of 2.2 billion DNA base pairs and 18,500 genes, was inconclusive. Nobody knew how or why or what had caused the platypus to be the amazing mix that it is.

---

1. "Platypus Genome Explains Animal's Peculiar Features; Holds Clues to Evolution of Mammals," *Washington University School of Medicine*, May 2008. Via *ScienceDaily*: http://www.sciencedaily.com/releases/2008/05/080507131453.htm.

And yet, this study did not stop the platypus from being, living, or enjoying itself as it walked around in its home down under! It did not stop the platypus from eating food with its duck-like bill, or waddling with its web feet, or recreating its progeny in platypus eggs.

In fact, the study affected the platypus in no way whatsoever.

We spend an inordinate amount of time in our young adulthood (or later on in life if we have been too busy going to school or raising a family or building a career in our young adulthood to tend to these questions) trying to figure out who we are.

What is our heredity? Who do we come from? What do we look like? What are our characteristics? What are our gifts? We try to plot and assess and figure out ourselves based on our likes, dislikes and characteristics... when really, none of it matters.

You may be man or woman. You may be of this race or that, or a mix of many races. You may have hair of any color, or no hair. You may be short, tall or in between. You may be from Europe, Africa, Asia, America, or anywhere else on earth. You may have a talent for music, dance, science, writing, or holding someone's hand.

None of this really matters.

Certainly, the particular mix of genomes that comprise you as a person make you unique—there's no one like you. But there's also nobody like anyone else. We're all unique—so what's the big deal?

When we stop looking at the particulars of our differences, and instead begin to see the particulars of sameness... this is where things get really interesting.

We're all as uniquely unique as anyone else, as anything else on the planet.

It's a passage of young adulthood in which we discover who we are, we claim our right to be different, we become concerned with who we are.

In later years, we are no longer concerned with this question, this way of sorting or separating ourselves into this category or that. We are happy enough, just to be.

———

Stop trying to determine who you are, stop trying to tell your story. Just let it rest, and find quiet gratitude for what and who you are. Instead of trying to look at all the ways you are different from everyone else, or unique, or special, simply be your own platypus, a mix of everything. Be grateful that we are a mix of everything.

10

Finding our true skin

There comes a time in every teen's life when they move from the Peanuts and Hello Kitty pre-teen T-shirt section of Old Navy to the more glamorous teen section where the shirts are ruffled and lacy and mysterious, not really T-shirts at all.

That day was today.

Amidst the 4th of July specials we journeyed, looking askance at anything red, white, or blue.

Instead, the shopper in question, now 12.75 years, settled on a cardigan and skirt, as previously noticed in her copy of *Teen Vogue*.

If you have ever waited in an Old Navy with the disco pop blaring, while your almost-a-teen tries on 368 items of clothing… perhaps you have not really lived.

In the end, what she chose was absolutely perfect for the person she was becoming. No longer a girl, but still a long ways from woman.

A kid who still liked Converse and hoodies . . . but who wanted to look different this year.

A new match, for the being now emerging.

She worked fast, quickly dismissing everything that did not fit, did not work, and handed those out of the dressing room door so that I, as Mom, could put them back on the hangers, and hang them to be returned to the floor.

This process of finding our new skin is the same at any age.

We grow out of one aspect, one personality, one stage. We try on different aspects of ourselves, until we find what is most authentic, what is most interesting, what fits the best. We will put on many skins, and we will discard many skins in this lifetime, as we pare down to reveal our true inner self.

It is well worth the time and effort, however long this journey takes.

————

Think about who you were ten years ago. Twenty. Think about how you were raised and who you are now. Think about the skin you are in now, and if it still feels comfortable to you. Have you just taken on a new skin or are you in the midst of shedding an old one?

11
Tethered

When I was a kid, I ran free. As a girl of ten, I rode my bike mile after mile into the surrounding neighborhoods, to the parks and schools and stores where all the other kids hung out.

There were no rules. There were no cell phones. There was a nickel and a dime that you might grab from the coin dish on the top of your dad's dresser and slip into your sneaker—enough to make a phone call from a phone booth along the way, in case of an emergency.

There were no area codes creating a nine-digit number, either. There were letters and numbers, a combination of seven, total. If you called from certain phones, there would be others already having a conversation; a party line, it was called. You'd need to wait your turn.

We walked, we traveled, we journeyed. We rode our bikes, and we rode on the backs of each other's bikes: sitting on handlebars, standing on the back while the other sat and pedaled. We were free, in a way that free is not possible for a child of ten or twelve in America to live now.

In these times, I feel vulnerable if I step outside without my cell phone. What if I need to call someone? What if I have a car problem? What if, what if, what if?

The truth is, this continuous tethering to one another via technology has changed us. We no longer trust ourselves to be safe and whole as we are out in the world. We think we'll be alone if we don't have the continuous tethering of the cell phone whenever we are walking, biking, driving.

I rarely used the nickel and dime from my sneaker, back then. Instead, I simply sensed the time by the shadow of the trees, by the way the birds swooped in the air. More often then not, I knew when to come home when I saw a picture in my mind of my mother, calling me with her own mind from many miles away.

We're always connected, whether we have cell phones or not. We were then. We are now. It is the nature of the Universe.

———

Leave your phone behind today when you go out to do errands. See how you feel differently in the world. Do you feel safe? Do you feel nervous? See if you can recognize that you are still as connected and tethered to everyone you love, even without your phone. Relax into this connection, allow yourself to experience and be grateful for the natural tethers we are all provided, and know all is well.

12

Exhilaration

When I was young, I played soccer in Seattle. I remember my team practicing in the late fall afternoons until the ball became invisible, loping across the field until darkness encroached like a mist.

Fall is coming, the sky seemed to say. *Darkness is here.*

We grabbed as much light as we could, but by 7:00 pm, it was too dark to see anymore.

We gathered the balls in big net bags, tossed them into the back of coach's car, and scattered into the dark; some heading for cars, some getting rides.

"Need a ride?" someone called to me across the shadow-slanted field.

"Nope," I waved. "Got my bike."

It was the part of the practice I liked best. My body wobbly with the efforts of practice; tired in the best way. The field finally deserted. And nothing ahead but the cool ride home.

It was just six miles—but in the dark, it was magical.

I would mount my bike, adjust my helmet, and push off into the night.

At first, it was overwhelming: My legs, tired after practice, were wobbly at first, slow to rise to the challenge, the adrenaline request of freedom, momentum, exhilaration, the dazzling sense of riding home on a dark fall evening, everything noise and light and cacophony in the city traffic, while the darkness flew about my shoulders, the great mystery.

The first taste of freedom, the first experience of self in the world, the first taste of the great *I am* and the even greater *I am that*, and both simultaneously, is so sweet, so luscious and unexpected, that we find ourselves expanding at lightning speed—outside of our skin, outside of our mind, beyond our experience of consciousness.

This experience causes us to grow bigger than we've ever grown before.

Sometimes we cling to ourselves even as our self expands, even as if a great owl has swooped from the shadows, and for a moment we might imagine he has plucked us up in his talons.

Other times, we simply enter the mystery.

We shiver, cry out, pedal faster, laugh with the crazy amazement of it.

And then we let go, from the *I am*, into the *I am that*.

We are one, we are ourselves, and suddenly we have expanded past that, into Oneness. All this on an ordinary day when we are fourteen or fifteen or sixteen, riding with the mystery on a dark fall night, heading for the soft lights of home.

————

Recall an experience that gave you the sweet taste of freedom and expansion when you were fourteen, fifteen, sixteen. Perhaps it was your first time driving alone, your first job, or your first love. Go back into that memory today, and see what happens when you revisit it. We were all young once; we have all experienced this sudden expansion. Allow this memory to teach you gratitude for how exciting this life was then—and can be now.

13
Your future self awaits

There once was a young woman brought to me by her mother, because she would not go to school. In fact, she not only would not go to school, but she had not gone in several years.

> *Are you in school now?*
>
> No.
>
> *Did you go school last year?*
>
> A little.
>
> *The year before?*
>
> Yes, but it wasn't good.
>
> *The year before?*
>
> A little bit.
>
> *The year before?*
>
> No, I didn't go that year.

This girl, now a young woman, had not gone to school regularly for five years. She was now eighteen and as inconceivable as this might seem, she had received her high school diploma anyway. She did not know what to do next.

Her mother sat anxiously in the room with us, love and worry emitting from every part of her body, waiting to hear what I saw, what the guides might say, what information there was for this young woman who by all normal standards, by the standards of the college boards and the job market had made a muck of her life.

Yet that's not what the guides said at all.

I asked her to close her eyes and breathe deeply, and she went in very fast. I took notice right way, as often young people are incredibly psychic, incredibly spiritual beings, and from the way she entered in so quickly, I knew this to be the case.

The guides came crowding into the room, and I relaxed. This was going to be easy! Sometimes people get nervous entering in, or sometimes they resist. Sometimes they're afraid of what they'll find, and sometimes they already know what they're going to find and they don't want to hear it! This young woman was not stuck in this way. She was fully plugged in.

I asked her to imagine herself at age thirty, an impossibly old age for such a young person to envision. I asked her to tell me what she was doing there, where she was living, who she was living with, what she did for work.

She answered the questions at lightning speed.

An apartment.

With my boyfriend.

I'm working as a graphic designer.

We explored this future possibility of herself for a while, and then when I was satisfied she had looked around enough, I brought her back to the present moment. Sometimes when we are unclear, the future viewing of ourselves brings the present into focus: it shows us that where we are not is not where we will always be.

Wherever we are in this moment—in whatever place of chaos or confusion or uncertainty or pain, in whatever place of not believing we fit in, or not finding our way, whether we are eighteen or eighty— these are temporary places. Over time, we move through the awkward phases of ourselves, and into who we truly are.

This young woman did not go to school because deep in her core she knew it was not for her. Her sensitivity, shyness, and deep aware-ness were not well received in the public school system; she had suf-fered, and finally her soul said "no more."

There is life after school.

Sometimes, we just need to wait out one stage, where we are not able to put ourselves in the right place until the next stage comes. We seek our true selves always—this is the place to which the Divine con-tinually brings us.

———

Whether you did well in school, or did not do well, let these memories drift into your mind now. Release all judgment on your past achievements or failings. Let the pain relax from all memories, and understand that the present time is new and fresh, and realize thankfully that you are moving toward your true self.

14

Bloom when you're ready

There's a particular rose bush that sweeps over an archway in our garden. For most of the year, it's just a mass of green. But at some point, a profusion of tightly held buds shows up almost overnight

One day there's just leaves—you could go out with a magnifying glass, and no bud would be there. The very next day, you can't see anything but the buds; they're everywhere, the branches are laden.

It's just a matter of time.

During the last weeks of June, when the buds are preparing to bloom, I might head out there every afternoon, looking for the tell-tale signs of pale white petal.

But it's like waiting for popcorn to pop on the stove. All you can do is heat the oil, stand clear—and after waiting what seems like an eternity, you take your attention away for one second, and suddenly popcorn is flying wildly around the kitchen, while you madly race to find a cover.

The roses are like that too. Blooming when we least expect it.

One day after we've tired of searching the buds to see if they've opened, we'll awaken to the sweetest, most heady perfume wafting in through the open windows...the roses have bloomed, and it is a delirium of scent and color and beauty.

People are like this too.

One minute you're tight in the bud. The next you're exploded into beauty, fully expanded in yourself.

This happens repeatedly in your life, over and over again. Bud to bloom. Always in the timing that is exactly right for you.

———

Are you in the bud? Are you waiting to bloom? Consider what or how or when you will be blooming next. Be grateful for this process of life, in which you are repeatedly asked to grow, open, and bloom...

Part Three:
Connection

....

*In which we discover who is
accompanying us on this journey.*

15

Portal of miracles

As I stood before the sacred wall, its crumbling lava rock tangled with weeds, I was entranced by the view before me: dazzling blue ocean below, misted volcano above, the breeze itself whispering secrets from another time.

Suddenly, I saw this place as it had once been: laboring women trudging heavy up the mountain, midwives in attendance, and babies, red-faced and indignant as they crowned forth into dawn.

Here was *Pohaku Hoohanau*, ancient birthing place of Kaua'i, where the royals had come to bring their babies forth centuries ago. A place of hope, of miracles—of new souls welcomed to the world.

My attention was directed to a small green bundle tucked into the rocks. As soon as I saw it, the voices rushed in: *"Please, let my sister get better." "I'd like a baby, I've been waiting so long." "I need to do well in school, my parents are counting on me." "I got fired, and I haven't told my husband* yet." "I want to contact my mother." "I'm ready to meet my true love." "My heart is broken." "I need $200 to make it through the end of the month." "My husband's drinking is worse." "My legs aren't working." "I want to say thank you." "I miss my wife, I want to join her soon."

As these voices rose in this particular energy vortex, I saw that this ti leaf bundle was not the only one—the entire wall was filled with them. I was at an altar of sorts, a portal where the longings of the human heart might be easily conveyed to the Universe with each humble, ti-wrapped offering.

Kaua'i is like this: high vibration, Divine vibration, a place where the sacred trumps the mundane. There are other places like this on earth—vortices where the energy is more clear, where the veil is thinner, where we are more easily able to slip sideways in time, to communicate with those in the different layers and levels.

On this day, standing before the crumbled altar of ti leaf wishes, as the breeze whispered gently off the ocean and past mingled with the present, time overlapped time, I understood that this sacred place was here for all of us; we are not separate, but one soul with relationships that extend beyond the reaches of present, past or future.

All of us, so different from each other—yet in all times and in all histories, our desire to live in connection and with love is unquenchable.

It is so everywhere, for everyone.

———

What wishes do you have for the Universe? What would you like help with, or what do you need to know? Who has gone from this earth that you'd like to speak to again? Who in your family would you like to help? Today, find a private place, your own altar, and speak your whisperings to the cosmos. Wait to hear the answer, in that moment, or in the next few days. Give thanks for what is revealed.

16
The red thread

According to Chinese legend, the gods tie an invisible string around each of us at the ankle. The other end of this string is tied to those we are destined to know. We might call it the red string of fate. The red thread of destiny.

This magical cord may stretch or tangle, but it will never break. Not in this life, into the next life, nor into all the past or future.

We look at the red thread on our ankle and see who we are attached to. Sometimes, if you have come to a place in your life, you will laugh when you do this: everyone in your house may be attached to each other at the ankle by this red thread, regardless of whether one is in the bathroom, one in the kitchen, one working in the yard.

And yet, there are also those we meet so briefly, we forget that we may have red strings, cords, and threads with them too.

These connections are awaiting us when we least expect them. They are a kind of remembrance of karma, these red threads; a karma of helping, when we need it most:

The woman who holds the door open for us when we are struggling to carry a sleepy toddler; the man who moves over so we have a place to sit on the bus; the child who waves to you from a passing car, brightening your day; the doctor who uses intuition, not just science, to make your diagnosis; the traveler you meet in a far-off country who gives you shelter for the night and points you in the right direction in the morning.

The person we keep running into, over and over again, before we know this person is our soul mate.

These soul circles, soul connections—they last beyond time. If you close your eyes and ask to see the red threads, you will see a world filled with people with the dark red threads tied to their ankles, attached to someone else's ankle, and so on and so on.

In this way, no one is not attached. No one is free from the red thread. No one is alone in the Universe.

At first glance, this idea of the red thread may seem different from the idea of oneness, of being part of the One/Divine/All/Universe/God. But it's not. It's just another way of looking at it. In our attachment to each other, we are not separate. Not in this lifetime, not in any another.

Look today for the red threads that bind you to another infinitely and eternally. Honor the connections you have to another.

Who are you most tightly corded to, with the red thread in your life? Who are you on earth to help, and be helped by? Make a list of these people. Say a prayer of thanks for their presence in your life; that you have found them in this lifetime, and are in close and loving proximity.

—

17
At table

Wandering in after a long day, we bring it all with us: everywhere we've been, everyone we've been around. All our thoughts, worries, anxieties, and irritations tromp right along with us.

We take off our shoes in the mudroom, throw our jackets on our beds, sling our backpacks and purses on the floor, and before there is time to shower or read or relax in any way, we huddle together around the dining room table, all of us at the same time.

It's a hard transition.

A battlement of energies, from the four, sometimes five or six souls, at the table. It's easy to argue, complain, or retreat in irritation. But still we do it: we join hands, or at the very least we touch fingers and say the grace that comes to one of us:

Thank you. We acknowledge this time together.
Keep us safe. Let us have more days on this earth.

We are grateful.

The older souls around our table understand that it will not always be the same. Some will leave this soul circle, as some already have: The daughter to the California coast. The son who will move to college. The younger daughter who will also make her way.

The circle we have at today's table is not constant. It is always in flux. This is just a moment in time in which you pass the bread, pass the butter, and look at each other's faces in absolutely wonderment that you have been given the gift to be with them. To experience them. To love them.

In the family of your own childhood, you sat with different souls. Nothing is the same. We are always in change.

The circle you hold now, whether it is family, friends, or partner, or you yourself at table alone. The table becomes our Mecca's call; a place to stop, sit, and reflect on our day, lives, and on those we love.

———

What were the tables of your childhood like? Remember who sat around them with you. Now, think about the time you most recently sat at table. Recall who was there, and who you wished was there. If you are able, call them on the phone, or send a text or email. If you are not able, hold them close in your heart with gratitude for the times you were together.

18
The karma of pie

I made a pie for my family this weekend. The first wedges of cinnamon'd apple were gone before the pie was cool; it had vanished entirely by Sunday morning.

When you make a pie, you're tying back into a long line of pie-making, entangled back into the karmic threads of your ancestry. At least for me it is.

My mother did not make pies, but my grandmother did: her family immigrated from the green hills of Ireland at the turn of the twentieth century, finding themselves somehow settled in the flats of Missouri and Nebraska. Their red hair stood out on the plains. Their freckles even more.

My grandmother had her first child at sixteen, and nine more after that. Six of them survived, with the last one, my mother, being born at the height of the Depression.

My grandmother kept a garden all summer long, and chickens in the yard, and this is how the family ate. She also worked full time as a photographer's helper: developing film, processing prints, doing the hand-tinting that was popular at the time—well before the age of Instagram, 300 dpi, and Photoshop.

My grandmother was busy! So making a pie took on a sort of sacred event status—reserved for Sunday lunch. Her pie, made early in the morning so it would have time to cool, only made it once to the table before it was devoured down to crumbs.

My grandmother lived on the west coast for a while. During this time, when I was small, she taught me to bake, and one of the things we baked was pie.

"There's a secret to the crust; I've never been able to get it right," she'd tell me as we chopped the cold butter into the flour.

"The rolling always sticks for me," she'd confess as we rolled the cold crust.

It was reassuring to have my grandmother tell me where she'd failed, pie wise, as we worked together, even thought her crust seemed impossibly flaky, her rolling pin always clean. I followed along as best I could, anticipation building as the oven steamed and baked.

But when it came to the taste, I found out something interesting: I didn't like pie—neither apple nor peach nor coconut cream.

In other words, I liked the making, but not the eating.

This weekend, I made the pie with the help of my youngest daughter, now twelve. I cut the apples, letting the peels spiral out with delightful magic. I sprinkled the sugar and dotted the butter. But when we got to the crust, it was she who rolled it out and constructed the pie: top layer, bottom layer, pinching the edges tight together and adding a tiny heart crust on top. The pie was perfect: flaky, golden, divine.

We inherit many things from our ancestors: karma, looks, and apparently, pie baking. My daughter, three generations down from my grandmother, was a phenomenal pie baker.

———

What have you inherited from your parents? Your grandparents? Your great-grandparents? Think back to the stories you know about these people who created you. Look at their pictures. Imagine their lives. What part of them are you especially grateful for? What still lives on in you or your children?

19.

What a soul needs to do

In third grade, my oldest daughter did a report on Cuba for her social studies class; she had to make a poster with pictures, and give an oral report. She always excelled at oral reports, the kind of kid who liked to plan elaborate costumes and take on a personality for her presentation.

For this presentation, she dressed as Fidel Castro.

It is funny to see a third grader dress up as most anything but to see her dressed as Fidel, complete with beard and cigar and hat, was really something. The thing is, she was not making fun of Fidel by taking on his character. Something about this person, this personality, this leader of a small country that was quite different than the rest of the world, caught her imagination—in fact, I would say it caught her soul.

From third grade on, Cuba became her obsession—she learned Spanish, which is a common enough language to learn where we live. But she didn't just learn it by the book, by rote, just enough to get her language requirements out of the way. Instead, she learned to speak it fluently, and she entered college as a Spanish major, so she could read and speak the language, and understand the many cultures of these countries.

When she was twenty, my daughter was invited to be a part of a select group of about ten students who would go to Cuba. At the time, Cuba was off limits to Americans, so this was a big deal, a major achievement.

And, being her mother, I was adamant that she not go—I fought, I resisted, I threatened. Being over the age of eighteen, she blithely ignored me, arranged her passport, all her flights, vaccinations, and tickets, and off she went for six months.

Sometimes, a soul knows what a soul needs to do. I do not know if my daughter had a past life in Cuba, but she was drawn to this place, this country, these people as if she had lived there forever.

There are photos of my daughter, a thin girl with long golden hair, walking through a barrio with little kids following her. She's playing soccer with boys on the street. She's swimming in the ocean with her arms uplifted in the waves in pure bliss and exultation. The images capture a person with a kind of openness and joy that I would call spiritual love—she is brimming forth with it. In other photos, she's playing cards with old men and old women on their front stoops. She's chatting at length with the maids who come to clean her student room. She's got a crowd of people in her room, all waiting to use her (rare) computer and Internet connection. She's attending national soccer games. She's in college, and all of the books and tests and papers are all in Spanish. She's falling in love.

When my daughter had to leave Cuba, it was very difficult for her. There is something that happens when you finally arrive at a place that your heart has called you to for so many years, and then you must leave that place, not knowing when you will ever be able to return.

The restrictions seem to be relaxing. And people do go to Cuba by way of Canada, Mexico, and South America. But today, she is a broke student living in the U. S., and Cuba remains in Cuba.

I'm not an avid traveler; I don't long for long plane flights and lugging backpacks. But my daughter is keen to see as much of the world as she can. Directly after Cuba, she traveled to Uruguay for another six months. When she is done with school, she plans to travel to the Himalayas, and then beyond.

Our souls must go where they are called to on this planet, whether you move in the realm of the spirit, imagination, and mind, or whether you move in the realm of physical travel on the earth plane.

————

Close your eyes. Breathe in through the nose and out through your mouth. Ask the Divine to show you the places on the planet that your soul calls for. You may see these places, these situations as something out of a past life memory. Or, you may see your soul directing you to travel to these places now, in this lifetime. If you are directed to travel to a place on this planet, do not wait. Life is meant to be experienced fully. The gratitude that will come into your heart from this journey will overwhelm and transform you.

20

Tenderheart

Sometimes the children we bring into the world look so much like us, have so many of our characteristics, that we think that they are the same as us.

But sometimes they are better: More advanced. More enlightened. Further along.

It is true, we live in enlightened times: the new generations represent notches on the belt of evolution, to be sure. It is true that we know how to parent better than we did generations ago, and this leads to healthier, more developed children who can go further than we could.

But to have these magic beings show up in your house, marching around like little spiritual teachers at the tender ages of four and five … this can set a parent back in her tracks.

It requires a lot of humility, a lot of strength and the understanding that the best is actually going to be good enough to deal with these little mini teachers in the making.

Every great spiritual teacher, every great *bodhisattva*, saint, or guru was a child once. And while growing up, there was maturation at two levels—the level of the spiritual being, in which consciousness expanded rapidly and easily, and at the level of the earth being, in which things like school and homework and picking up dirty socks left behind the bed for far too long present the more immediate challenges.

All of my children are spiritual teachers, but the one who is currently having the most struggle with earth life is my youngest son, now seventeen.

He's fine spending hours in nature, meditating, or simply sitting. He's wonderful in music, writing songs on his guitar, and singing. He loves to dance, and he loves martial arts. But the things we traditionally are concerned about for junior year really leave him cold: school work, school activities, the whole high school scene.

It's as if he's just trying to get through it so he can move on to his real life, his true calling.

When he was little, a kid of four or five who never was without a stick in his hand, who would sleep with a collection of sticks under and *in* bed with him, we used to call him Big Heart or Tenderheart, like the name you might have found stitched onto a Care Bear, back in the day.

He's a warrior and a protector, and his heart brims for the underdog, the vulnerable, the wounded in this world. His heart sees clearly the great injustices of the world. He has no patience for bigotry, igno-rance, or acting without ethics in the world. His spiritual understand-ing is so clear, he had trouble understanding why everyone cannot see it this way.

It is a hard time, being stuck in a time and place when you are un-able to move fully into your authentic self, your soul's calling. Just a few decades ago, he would have been considered a man for several years—he would have been out riding the range, or working or exploring or all the other myriad ways a young man can take his destiny into his own hands.

In this time and place, he is still not eighteen, and I sit and watch and wait, holding patience in my hand like a small bird, trusting life will unfold soon for him; that his life's path will be as grand and mystical and wondrous as he has already foreseen.

———

Think back to yourself at seventeen. Recall again how stuck you were, or how free. What were you doing? What did you long for? What meant more to you than anything else in your life back then? Chances are good that there's a lot of this longing left in you now. Be grateful for the passion of your youth. Allow your passionate self to guide you to more authentic, deeper, and richer living starting today.

21

Walking the tightrope

When you raise a few kids, you get used to spotting the signs that your child is doing okay. You know what they're supposed to be learning. You track the important milestones. You know the developmental rites of passage.

By the time your youngest begins her passage from infant to independent being, you think you've found your groove as a parent—you no longer panic on First Day of Kindergarten, even though you might still shed a few tears. You no longer flip out when your child tells you she needs a full banana costume, complete with yellow tights by tomorrow morning, and it is now 10 pm. You know how to bring down a fever, ease a queasy stomach, and host a sleepover.

You're experienced. You've been through it all. Nothing's going to come up that you haven't seen before. Except of course, this is not true.

When my youngest daughter was born, she weighed 10 pounds, 4 ounces. She was born naturally, without an epidural or drugs, and when the huge glorious heft of her was ready to come out, she got stuck. Her head crowned, but her shoulders were too broad. The doctor, after commanding me to push, then stop, reached her deft, capable hand up inside me *almost like a vet would do for a cow*, I remembered thinking later, and wrenched my daughter out. Six month later, my daughter was dropped in a family mishap that included a series of events, and broke her arm. I saw her arm hanging funny off of her shoulder, and to the emergency room we went.

I don't know if these two events relate to what came later; it's hard to know these things. I'm just telling the story.

Things went along without further mishap until the summer of my daughter's eleventh year, when we got a massage table for home. It was an absolute beauty, carved in rosewood with a beautiful rose padding. My daughter was crazy about it, and pestered me day and night to give her a massage. I was busy that summer, and kept saying no, or later, or all the things parents say.

But she would not give up.

When she finally lay down on the massage table, I immediately noticed something funny about her right shoulder. It was sticking up, or perhaps it was sticking out. It didn't look right. I tried to press it down as I did the massage, but it didn't budge.

My partner, a chiropractor, took one look at my beautiful, lovely eleven-year-old daughter lying there on the new massage table, and the next day we were getting x-rays.

The curve was there in black and white; indisputable. Scoliosis. An aggressive, major curve.

We tried every kind of holistic therapy. We did chiropractic, massage, yoga, physical therapy, prayer, and visualization. "I'm getting the surgery, Mom," my daughter declared at all our efforts, "It's going to fix my back."

A year later almost to the day, about twelve of us sat in the waiting room at Randall Children's Hospital in Portland—an entire support group of blended family—while my youngest daughter had an eight-hour surgery to straighten her spine. Two rods were put in her back permanently, and many titanium screws. She was in the hospital for six nights, and I slept there on the trundle bed in the room.

She walked a distance of ten feet three days later and you probably heard the cheers of delight from her family from where you are living now! Just a few months later, and she's doing marvelously—three inches taller, healthy, with a beautiful back with a scar down the middle, that in one year will be fused enough to allow her to play sports, dance, and run.

Sometimes you think you know what to look for. Sometimes things take you by surprise. Living this life is like walking a tightrope over Niagra Falls—not just once, but continually back and forth, back and forth. There is no getting to the other side. There is just hanging up there in the breeze, and being grateful you are still standing.

———

What miracles have you experienced in your life? Think now about the big events, the medical events, the emergencies that turned out well. Close your eyes, and be grateful for the actual gift of living and breathing another day, another minute. Allow these thoughts to bring thanks and joy to your heart.

22

Catching beauty

The temperature had been dropping all day. It was a few days or so after Christmas, but not yet the new year, and we'd just returned from our holiday travels up to Washington. Just like every year, we'd packed the car and the kids and the presents and the dogs, and then returned with everything the same, except the presents we'd given had been left in Seattle, and the presents we received were now being taken home. We pack orderly going up, and then we shovel everything in pell-mell on the way home.

If you have ever traveled I-5 in a Honda Pilot filled with three older kids, two dogs, and way too many presents, everyone groggy from too much holiday food and variable sleeping arrangements and not enough exercise, you know this is not the most fun experience in the world.

We'd been back a few days and were enjoying the remainder of Christmas vacation in the most splendid way our family could imagine:

we were doing nothing. We were sleeping in late, and staying up later watching movies, and taking luscious walks in the woods around our house in the afternoon. The house was warm and dry, and the power had not yet gone out this winter. We felt lucky, easy, and happy.

When the snow came that night, it was a surprise. The forecast had predicted it would come next morning, but here it was at bedtime: thick and plump and in full flurry, as if somebody had just decided to turn on a giant snow machine upstairs. It was as if orbs of light were descending from the sky, millions and millions of them.

The kids began to scream and shout in excitement; snow was something they'd never seen in their respective years on earth (they were then eleven, sixteen, and twenty). They pounded downstairs and piled into whatever coats and jackets were on the hooks in the mudroom. They scampered outside under the great fir trees and danced happy dances and sang "White Christmas" and mucked around, making snowballs out of the drifts of snow that were already beginning to gather on the driveway.

We watched them for a while, then snuck away to the open back porch, where we bundled in blankets and sat in the deck chairs that swiveled and watched the snow whirl around us like madness, like beauty, like grace. The snow danced and flew and skipped and we sat there laughing and sticking out our tongues to catch it, holding hands and wondering at it: the great surprise, the sudden, sheer sweetness of this event in our lives, dropping out of the sky unexpectedly, and here we are in the midst of this dance, this whirling waltz of dark and light.

This year, it is likely we will make the trip to Washington again, packing up the car with kids and presents. As of yet, there is no sign of snow. But the deck chairs have found a permanent place on our back porch in case of unexpected beauty meant to be watched, rejoiced, celebrated, and danced with, on any given day to come.

———

There is beauty in every day and in every season. Grace arrives to us, plops down right in front of us, whether we noticed it or not. Today, bear witness to something extraordinary. Catch some beauty. Often, all this requires is being still and watching with newly thankful eyes.

Part Four:
Love

....

In which we discover our Beloved,
our true soul companion.

23
We hear with our skin

There was a study done in which it was discovered that we do not just hear with our ears.[2] We also hear through our skin.

Of course, if you've been to a rock concert where the bass and the beat have vibrated down to bone, you know this already. If you've stood in an ancient church when the cantor's voice soared into the arc of the cathedral so pure and clear that the hair stood up on your arms, this is nothing new to you.

But this study was less visceral, more practical, an earnest attempt to empirically prove in the way science finds so necessary. The experiment involving puffs of air hitting the skin while the participants listened to simple syllables. When it came down to the tallied results,

---

2. Bryan Gick and Donald Derrick, "Aero-tactile Integration in Speech Perception," *Nature* 462, (2008).

the participants heard the puff, not the sound. In other words, we don't just hear. We don't just see. We perceive with our whole body.

We see sound. We hear light. We feel everything.

We perceive, sense, intuit, know. The whole Universe of information is available to us at all times. This is consciousness in the human body.

When we use our third eye, our intuitive eye, we see things that are beyond the realm of our current reality. We perceive the energy of all time, all space, beyond all boundaries of what we expect.

Every cell of us knows everything.

Scientists can't prove this entirely, empirically, in the way science likes to prove things, yet. But it's coming.

————

Close your eyes. Cover your ears. Perceive with your skin. Do you understand how you know everything even without the seeing, hearing, touching? Be thankful for the way consciousness truly works, making everything available to you at all times.

24
True loves

The idea that we're only going to love once in our life is just not true.

We're designed to love as deeply as we can, from the first moment of birth when we look into the eyes of the first person we see, and that's it—we're head over heels, swooning to connect with another soul.

The love we're capable of isn't always romantic love. As infants and children, we love other beings passionately: our mother, our father, our dog.

But as we get older, we begin to search for our true mate, the destined Beloved who will join with us on our pathway through adulthood. To build a family, perhaps. Or to create a haven and home when the world gets rocky. Or to explore different parts of our personality, or our work in this world.

The thing is—there's not just one love out there. Now, you may be one of those rare people who meet your love in high school and stay together for decades. But for most of us, a number of soul mates will arrive; most of us will find true love with more than one person over time. This may include an early relationship in our teens. Another relationship in young adulthood. Another relationship in the middle years. Perhaps even another, as we get old.

In all of these loves, there will be one you will think of as the Beloved, the true soul mate. But in fact, all these soul connections are important. All of these are of value. All of these are to be held with extraordinary gratitude in our hearts, no matter if they've ended with ease and respect, or with great chaos and wounding.

We love at the depth we are capable of at the time. When we are young, we love with passion, energy, and the thrill of everything new. When we are in the middle years, we believe we know who we are, and may attempt to choose someone who fits this idea of our self. When we've have reached later life, we've experienced so much that we may choose a different kind of person still.

These loves of our lives who we discover early, middle, late? They're all miracles. There's not a mistake among them. All of these relationships, these soul matings, allow us to grow fully into the beings we are becoming.

———

If you've been divorced or ever had a relationship that left you wounded, bring this person into your mind now. Let go of all the grievances you have toward this person—just let them go. Consider that you entered this relationship for a reason, and allow the reason to now come into your mind. Take a deep breath and give gratitude for all your life experiences. Understand the great gift of all the people you have loved in all the ways you have loved them.

25
Coming home

When you meet your soul mate, your Beloved, you can't remember life before him or her. The way your life becomes magnified and mingled and magnificent in the presence of this person is different than anything you've ever known. It's like coming home.

Sometimes it takes many years before this person appears to you, or before you are ready to meet this person. In my case, I was forty-two. At the time, the divorce of my marriage was still in progress, involving excruciating meetings with the mediator as the details were hammered out. After eighteen years of marriage, we were living separately for the first time, with much strain and awkwardness. It was insanity, a crazy time of releasing into what was new without much grace, closure, or comfort for anyone. It was like walking around with a giant wound open to the world ... each day was painful.

During this time, my spiritual awakening had also begun in full force. Spirit guides had started to float through my new living room. I was receiving spiritual teachings in channeled writing. My body was in the throes of Kundalini or energy awakening almost every day. My old self had collapsed like a black hole, and the birthing of the new self was difficult—a hard labor.

Into this chasm of pain, sadness, opening, I met my Beloved, my true soul mate. The one I had been waiting for my whole life.

I met him in a writing group and although I do believe in love at first sight, I did not "see" him for many weeks! For one thing, he was wearing a disguise: a long beard, hair past his shoulders, and a type of clothing that I would call Oregon casual. He seemed much older than me, even though he wasn't. In fact, my only impression of him in those early days was that he was "a nice man," "really smart," and a "good writer."

I did not find it odd that at the end of each writing group, while everyone else was saying their goodbyes, he would turn to me and hug me goodbye—I just thought he was a hugger; some people are like that. I sank into his hug, a moment of relief, calm, and extreme comfort in the midst of my life's chaos. I took it as a gift, nothing more.

Each week, we met at a small room in the back of a coffee shop, crowded into the far booth with chairs added to fit everyone, and we exchanged our writing—I gave my novel to everyone in class to read, and person X gave her poems, and person Y gave his song lyrics, and this man gave his short stories.

Each person would read aloud from his or her work, and then we would all make comments—hopefully constructive ones. On one of these days, I looked up as this man read his work aloud to the group. A nice man, a good hugger, sitting directly across from me in the booth. He had just put on his reading glasses. And as I looked across at him in that moment, the Universe seemed to swerve into a new place, and my mind said: *He has the most beautiful face I've ever seen.*

As I stared in shock, at this man from my writing group whom I did not know, my mind said: *This is the man I love...*

Nine years later, he still tells the story of how he was smitten with me from the first day we meet—how I stuck out my hand to shake his and he flew over the moon in love as his mind told him: *This is the woman you have been waiting for.*

Nine years later, he still tells me how he waited for weeks until he was certain I understood this too, because he knew if he acted too early, I would have run away forever.

Nine years later, I know I have been blessed with the gift of love in this lifetime. With this man I have written books, recorded music albums, created teachings, raised our blended family, lived in a magical home in the woods, and had the most complete relationship I've known.

It's like coming home.

The problem in meeting your true love later in life is that you don't know how much time you'll have together. However, this is illusion. With true love, one moment is more than you will ever need;

eternity is not enough. In true love, you understand that no one else is out there for you in this cosmos, in this lifetime or in the next.

———

If you have found your Beloved, I implore you to recognize this as the gift it is. If you have not found this person yet, don't stop seeking. In every lifetime, there's a moment when you will come home. If it has not happened to you yet, it is a great gift still waiting to be opened and received with thanks.

26

Becoming luminous

Some things happen once in a lifetime. For whatever reason, we find ourselves in the right place at the right time with the right person to bear witness to the exact miracle we are witnessing.

These convergences, in which all the elements come into play with the precision of Swiss clockwork, happen to us millions of times a day. But it is only when we pay attention, when we see with clear eyes that we are able to witness these miraculous, unexpected events.

Years ago, I was on the beach at Puget Sound—a small, secluded beach where it's common to spot eagles soaring overhead in the spring. In the summer, salmon flip over waves, their silver bellies flashing. In the winter, the mountains in the distance shine with white snow.

It's in the fall that things glum up: they go all gray and gloomy, so misty that your clothes hold moisture for months at a time.

It was one of those days, October maybe, or November, that I found myself sitting on a piece of driftwood, a giant tree trunk gone silvery dark with sea air and salt, in a down coat (highly unsuitable for the wet weather; it would soon go sodden), with no mittens and no hat (I'm not sure I even own them). Already, my hair was curling from the moisture, and pretty soon it would be wet, dripping with the rain that seemed to condense upon us with every minute.

It was night, and our plan was to drum, my partner and I, on the beach.

Our plan had started out as a very good idea—he is a musical savant, able to play any instrument almost just by looking at it, and drumming is one of his fortes. I'm not a good drummer, but he doesn't seem to mind. We thought it might be "fun"—a word I used a lot back then and still use a lot now—to drum on the beach in the foggy moonlight.

After lugging two heavy African djembe over a quarter mile of wet sand, it seemed a little less fun.

After having to move from our spot three times because the first two times we inadvertently sat too close to the place on the cliffs where there was an eagles' nest, and the eagles had begun to screech at us in a threatening way, it seemed even less fun.

By the time we moved even farther down the beach, looking back over our shoulders for attacking eagles, I was wet, cold, and a little defeated. Finally, I just stopped where I was, plopped on a nearby driftwood log and said, "Let's drum here."

And we did drum for a few minutes—until it soon became clear that our hands were so wet that the drum heads were getting wet too, and the only sounds we could produce were alternately a slippery slide or a dull thump.

We sat there for a moment with the rain dripping down our foreheads, the moon full overhead, as the realization sank in that we were not having any fun at all.

And that's when my partner got up and started throwing stones into the ocean, heaving them far out at first, then skipping them in intricate shallow skips closer to the shore—and that's when we saw that the water was phosphorescent.

I'd only read about this phenomenon in books, the way the water trails green light, a luminescence caused by the presence of tiny ocean organisms, sometimes even crustaceans, jellyfish, or certain fish.

We did not know the source of this bioluminescence. Yet here it was in front of us, and I raced to the water see it for myself—to throw stones and watch the glowing circle of light create an aura in the waves, to trail a stick through and watch the green-white wake that formed behind it, and finally, to trail my fingers directly in the water and watch the light spark and dance.

We stamped our feet in the water, and laughed and shouted as flashes of green sparked before us. In this moment of light, in this experience of phosphorescence, our plans for drumming were instantly forgotten, and we were suffused with joy.

_____

Sometimes plans change. Sometimes we think we are being led in one direction, only to find that the Universe has been leading us toward something else entirely—an experience or understanding that we could have never directed or anticipated. Think back to a time when you made plans that changed unexpectedly. Recall the gift this unexpected change brought into your life.

27
The gift of sex

When I begin to see a pattern or a clustering in the questions that people are asking, a little Divine warning signal starts beeping in my mind, and I begin to pay even closer attention.

Often the questions I am asked are common, because most times we're all going through the same basic human situations over and over again:

What is my life's path? What is my life's purpose? What is my life's work? How is my health? How can I heal? Am I having a spiritual awakening?

And of course, *when will I find my true love?*

Sometimes though, the questions cluster in such an insistent way that I am directed to look at the question from a new angle or new perspective.

For example, I recently received an email from a man in India, an email that at first I thought was a prank, joke, or even inappropriate:

"I have a problem with sex," he wrote. "I can't get it out of my mind."

The next day, in a client session with a young American man of twenty-three, the same question was asked:

"I can't stop thinking about sex. I don't know what to do about it."

And two days later, in session with a man of forty from South America:

"I seek my true spiritual companion, but with the women I meet, I feel nothing."

And later that same day, with a man of thirty-one from Egypt:

"I'm calling in my spiritual partner. I don't want to waste any more time. I think it's that woman (he points to a woman nearby, a woman of extraordinary beauty). Do you think it's her?"

I look at her and instantly know that this woman is so far from being his soul mate that I'm not even sure if she's in his soul cluster. He's captivated by her physical beauty, but the soul connection is so far from being activated, it confuses me how he cannot see this.

The energy of sex is powerful. We talk about tantra as a way to explore this. Kundalini is another way; people spend thousands of dollars on sexual connection workshops worldwide. Some of them on one end of the spectrum go to night clubs and discos to dance their sexuality; folks elsewhere go to ecstatic dance or yoga. Some watch pornography, some read erotic fiction, others are infused with it in magazines, video, and media of all kinds.

Some people are celibate—they desire to quench the fire. Others are promiscuous—they desire to burn the fire out. Some are sexually active in a committed way, either in marriage or in relationships. Some connect with the opposite sex, some with the same sex. Some procreate, some do not. There are so many ways to explore this power, this connection between one and another!

We talk about sexuality having gone awry in the mainstream, and it has: whether it is repressed by cultural or religious roots, or overly flaunted, such as we see in pornography culture and the media at large.

It's like we haven't figured out the sacred nature of sex. We think it's something dirty—when it's the deepest, most spiritual connection we can have with another human being. It's not just for recreation; it is a way of relating body to body, soul to soul, with another.

We have mostly forgotten that sexual energy at its highest level is Divine merging between beings.

This is energy at the highest level.

For many men—and to a lesser extent, women—sex and pornography and desire and love are all mixed up. They can't figure it out.

And yet each of the four men who spoke to me had the same question, put different ways:

I am obsessed with sex,

I am captivated by physical attraction, and

I am hungry for sexual connection,

was what they asked on the surface.

And yet at the same time, the deeper question was also there:

I want this spiritual experience of sex, the real thing.

I want my soul mate.

I want the highest level of connection possible.

Both questions: the profane and the sacred, all mixed up together.

When we reach a point in our lives where we can understand the true nature of sex: Divine merging of body to body, soul to soul … we begin to shift beyond the cultural misinformation and misrepresentation of this sacred connection. The joy and bliss that is possible in our sexuality—a part of ourselves that is no less ourselves than anything else in this earth container we call a body, this earth awareness we call thoughts, this sacred consciousness we call soul—it's then we start to appreciate the absolute gift this connection allows.

————

Reconsider your ideas about sex, the ideas you've been raised with, and the images the media presents to you. Instead, look at the beings around you not as just bodies, but as souls.

28

The shedding of skins

There is a moment in sex when you don't know who you are anymore.

It doesn't happen like this for everyone. Maybe it never happens for some. But for those who have found their Beloved, it is if you have taken off your skin at the moment in which you take off your clothes. You remove your own skin from some secret zipper or snap or button system in your epidermis. You slip off your skin and hang it over the bed frame and slide under the covers entirely naked, every nerve and blood vessel and cell exposed.

Except the body is not what is exposed.

It is the soul that slides open, skinless, exposed, like an open mouth waiting to be kissed, all hunger and yearning to be fully connected, if only for a moment, if only for the space of those few minutes when you dissolve and dissolve again with another … and come up delirious, weakened, awestruck.

Skinless, we become whole: our full and complete humility, the grace of our arms wrapping each other, the joining of our bodies in the most complete way a human can.

On earth, there is no other way. This is as close as we can get.

Getting naked—getting naked down to the soul—requires a trust in oneself, in your lover, in the Universe, that if you expose yourself at this level, you will be not be harmed or hurt.

When you are able to set aside all your skins of insecurity, fear, anxiety, shame, shyness, when you are able to take off all these outer layers and simply be with another, a new kind of consciousness enters the room.

In this way, God is also there. Not just two bodies, not just two souls. But all body, all soul, One.

———

Consider how much or how little you allow yourself to be exposed to your Beloved. Is your body connecting, but not your soul? How grateful might you be if you did allow this true nakedness with another—not just in body, but in your entire Divine being?

29
The feast

"It's calendula," my partner says to me, holding it out like an offering.

I looked at the bright curling flower held in the center of his palm, a tiny orange heart beating.

"Do you eat flowers?" he asks.

It's a small flower, softly petaled, with a froth of pollen inside the center, like a saucer of color. What's different from a daisy or black-eyed susan is this softness, the way these petals flutter and dip like eye lashes.

No, I think.

"They're good for healing," he notes easily.

It's a flower. Orange, bright, pretty. I might use this flower in an arrangement, a soft posy to float in a shallow bowl. I might string this flower in a small loopy garland, and drape it over a bed of moss. There are so many things I might do with this sweet, heartbreaking flower.

But eat it?

I stare at it in his hand. It's a flower. It's a food. Colorful as the bright red of an apple, the hot orange of a pepper, the crisp yellow of a lemon. Gaudy, hot, bright.

All it would take would be a sudden shift in perception to re-review this flower, to take it petal by petal and see it from another reality. As if the very act of believing that this was a flower, that this was also a food might allow me take this flower, detach a single bright petal and place it softly, easily on my tongue.

The flower could be a feast.

If only I could turn my mind one tiny millimeter, to see it from that angle. See. Eat. Feast.

Which I did. The petals were sweet in my mouth, the pollen like honey. A sense of happiness pervaded my whole body as I ate the flower.

If you can change the way you think, the paradigm shift, everything that you view will change. Not just the reality of the flower. But the reality that is the feast of life itself.

————

If the season is right, find a flower that is edible: nasturtium, calendula, dandelion, and practice looking at it as a flower, and knowing it also as a feast. Eat it slowly, and taste it. Look at everything in your life today, as being not only what it seems. Where is the feast for you, when you look this way?

30
Swing step

When I first began to write seriously, I rented a tiny writing office in a dance studio. Once used as a coatroom or changing room for dancers, the office was adjacent to the big room, its expanse of gleaming wood floor and barre along one wall. Now rented as facility space for a variety of programs, the former studio didn't need it.

On Mondays there was Pilates in the day, ballet in the afternoon, Irish dancing at night. On Tuesdays, there was Pilates in the day, tap in the afternoon, and ecstatic dance at night. And so it went during the week.

I used the tiny space, coat hooks still installed around the perimeter of the wall, in the times when the room would be quiet—in the morning when the studio was mostly still until the early afternoon when it got noisier, as the kids streamed in and the classes began.

On Fridays, the schedule was clear. The studio was invitingly empty, and I began to come to the space with great anticipation of a writing day undisturbed. I also loved the feeling of having the dance floor to myself, and would often bring my own music to dance uninhibited and alone in the enormous, high-ceilinged room. In fact, I began to count on coming in early on Fridays so I could have that delicious time to dance.

On the days that I did not remember to bring music, I would often dance simply to the music of the spheres—the music I heard in my own mind, the refrains that played out in my own soul.

One Friday, I was in the room dancing, when to my surprise there was a great banging at the locked front door. I stopped mid-whirl and went to open it. There stood an older couple carrying a boombox, demanding to be let in.

Let me clarify.

When I say older couple, I'm not using the age range that my kids might consider older, in their forties and fifties. When I say older couple, I'm not talking about an age range that I might consider starting to be older, in their eighties.

This couple was older, elderly. In fact, I was to learn in the next few minutes, the man, a tall, stooped, string bean of a man with ears so big they looked like another kind of appendage, was 103. The woman, a diminutive, slim lady covered in makeup and actually wearing a dancing dress, was much younger.

"I'm fifteen years his junior," she confided to me with great pride.

And then, to my surprise: "We're not actually married," she volunteered.

It took them a long time to put on their dancing shoes. They sat on the stage and she got her dancing shoes out of a small felt bag, and with great care put them on: Capezios, I thought, with a low heel. A pair she might have had for years.

He had a more difficult time of it, changing from the pair of sneakers he was wearing into what looked like a nearly identical pair of sneakers. But she was insistent, hovering over him.

It was hard for him to cross his leg up over his other leg to untie one shoe, and even harder to put on the other shoe, and then tie it. At one point I thought about going over to help, but then I hung back. It was clear they'd done this many times. I sat silent in my office with the door open into the studio, and observed.

When they were ready, they turned the boombox on and began to dance. It was "String of Pearls," and it was quite possibly the slowest, most beautiful swing step I've seen. His arms barely raised over her head as she stepped carefully into her turn, and he twirled her with gingerly caution, every step as fragile as if only their bones were dancing. They danced to three more songs, her face fierce with concentration. As the color rose into his face I began to worry if it was all too much.

When they were done, they walked carefully back to the stage and began the slow process of putting their shoes back on. They laughed a little and at one point he slowly, carefully kissed her on the cheek.

"We're here every week," the woman confided in me as they walked out through the front door. "We've been doing this for years."

I was confused as they left, knowing that they had never been here before on any Friday. They were not on the schedule, and in fact, I never saw them again. When I asked the studio director about them, she had no idea who they were.

And in this way, I began to wonder if perhaps they were real, if they were spirits, or perhaps in some time continuum, if they were both.

———

To dance with your partner at any age is a way to remind yourself of the longer dance of your lifetime together. Love does not end when we die; we continue the dance from the other realms. If you have not danced with your Beloved for a long time—say at a wedding, or other event—I invite you to dance with him or her today. Move slowly. Don't worry about the steps. Let the color rise in your cheeks.

Part Five:
Convergence

....

*In which we begin to gain an
awareness of miracles as reality.*

31

A simple slice of pizza

Sometimes you head out the door not having a clue as to why you're hurrying so fast, or dawdling so fiercely. Why would it possibly matter that you are on the road at 1:11 instead of 1:16? How does it make any difference that you're stopping at a coffee shop, or a bookstore, or a car wash?

Such is the nature of Divine convergence; the way in which the Divine places us, pushes us, prods us to be in the right place at the right time.

What is convergence? In earth reality, a coming together from different directions. In Universal reality, what happens when you find yourself in one place, and the other person finds him- or herself in the exact same place, at the exact same time.

It might not be another person, either.

It might be an animal, or an idea, or a thought, or an experience. It might be the words on the page of the book we suddenly reached for, without knowing why, high upon the shelf.

And the answer we had been looking for all day was finally found in those words.

We accept these convergences all the time. In fact, when we think about love, we *expect* them: that moment of staring across a crowded room and gazing for the first time to glimpse our Beloved.

We accept that a "meet cute" as they call it in the movies, is likely going to happen when it comes to romance. We're maybe a little bit upset if it doesn't happen that way.

But most often, Divine convergences don't have anything to with love. They're just as present when we're in need of finding something, or knowing something, or feeling something.

I remember once when a client, Amanda, could not decide where to go for dinner. It was after work, she was tired, and she headed for the neighborhood pub, usually an ideal spot for a Friday evening.

But when she rolled into the parking lot, something felt off. Not right.

"This is crazy," Amanda thought, grabbing her purse and marching purposefully to the pub door.

Yet even as she could smell the food on the grill wafting toward her, and her mouth watered for a cold beer, she was spinning around, heading back to her car and driving out of the parking lot.

"What was that about?" she muttered, now more tired and hungry than ever, with no idea where she was headed. She spotted a tiny pizza joint, a place she'd only been once before and hadn't liked at all. But she couldn't stop; she was heading there, almost as if angels were driving the car for her, as if an irresistible force was directing here there.

By this time, Amanda knew she was in the midst of a convergence, being pushed and pulled into a direction from where everything wonderful became possible.

Sure enough, there at the countering ordering slices was a woman she'd seen around town for years, but had never spoken to, Lila.

Lila smiled in vague recognition, and then inexplicably invited Amanda to eat with her. It was all as if it had been scripted from a Universal dream.

The two talked nonstop for the next hour, as if they'd known each other forever. When they finally parted ways, it was clear that something important had been started...

And it had. A year later, she and Lila had opened their first retail store in town, a gift store that focused on Lila's visual gifts and Amanda's understanding of business. Two years later, they had expanded: two retail stores, a gelato shop and a coffee shop in the making.

The two have become inseparable as friends and partners. Each seems to be a spark for the other, with the uncanny ability to fill in the gaps. And their collaboration, their convergence is golden: not just financially, but the way they spread good cheer to everyone who visits their stores and shops. It is the partnership of a lifetime. They both know it as such.

All because of a sudden, inexplicable stop at a pizza joint. All because Amanda followed the energy of convergence, swam in the flow—and the Universe did the rest.

———

The Universe is continually creating convergences for us: putting us in the right situation at the right time, so we will meet someone or experience something important to our soul growth. Think back over the last few days, to any time you began to notice the Universe managing your schedule. Do you see how the Universe is on your side, bringing you to higher and better possibilities than you yourself can imagine? Be grateful for this Divine assistance.

32
The young saint

It's late afternoon, and once again I've been working at an event all day. The crowd has slowed, and I'm thinking about packing up my booth for a while … but something compels me to wait.

So, I wait. I wait because something compels me, and I wait because in my mind I hear a voice say "wait" and I wait because when I write in my journal "is it time to leave?" the phrase is written instantly: "be still and wait."

And so, I wait.

A young dark-haired woman walks by and smiles, and I'm quite sure that she's not the one I'm waiting for. She's so young, she looks so happy and peaceful; surely she doesn't require my help.

There is no one else around, and I decide that instructions to wait or not, I'm ready to go. I stand to pack up my booth, and in a flash this woman has slipped into my chair, and she's smiling and laughing, the most relaxed and joyous being I've met in a long time.

She is from Mexico City, she says. She is taking a year off, for nothing else except to explore her spiritual path. She is traveling the world, in search of whatever it is that God would like to show her, tell her, have her understand. She has already traveled to California, Oregon, Washington, moving steadily north. She will go to Hawaii next week, and then to India.

She is traveling alone. She is twenty-eight with a tiny frame, and her glossy black hair is cut short so that she looks like a boy—a child, really. She is vulnerable, traveling in the world.

And yet it is clear that nothing has harmed her, that no ill will come to pass. She is absolutely protected at all times because of the grace of her being.

We talk for an hour, maybe more, about all that we have each seen, the spiritual experiences we have had, the way we understand things, and with every passing moment I realize that it is she who is the spiritual teacher to me. It is she who is the healer.

She had not been seeking me.

I had been waiting for her.

My vibration rises up and up and up to overflowing in the presence of this woman, this joyous and peaceful soul, as she speaks of what she has seen and what she has understood.

At long last we part as the dearest friends, the sweetest sisters, and she blesses me with fragrant oil from India, and she gifts me with a tiny quartz crystal, no bigger than the tip of my pinky. It is Divine illumination, this light that it emits.

Later that evening in my hotel room, and later yet on the road home, and even months later as I write this, this young woman comes into my mind, this young saint in the making.

I am so glad I waited.

———

We do not know when we will come in contact with a spiritual teacher, a person who lives with a foot in both worlds: etheric and earth. This can happen to us at any time, when we are relaxed, and open, and when we remember to wait. Today, wait thankfully for the miracle to arrive in your life.

33
Snow day

Once long ago I made plans to attend a music workshop at a local university. It was to be taught by a famous person—a highly lauded academic who would be traveling from back east; we would learn how to hear the rhythm within music. Not the beat or the count, but the soul of rhythm inside. I was thrilled and couldn't wait!

But on the morning of the workshop, I woke up to find it had snowed. Now, this was not a sprinkling or a light dusting. This was massive snow, the kind we sometimes get here where the snow begins secretly in the wee hours, and it's a foot by morning.

I debated back and forth whether to go or not, finally decided to skip it, and then had that weird feeling in my stomach of discomfort with my decision. I always follow those feelings, even if I don't know why. I chained up the car and drove slowly into town, navigating the icy roads to campus.

The university was in storm emergency; staked out with "Do Not Cross" barriers and caution tape. The campus architecture was designed with steep modern roofs, and as I walked along the detour, ice slid and crashed in enormous jagged sheets of thirty feet or more; an ominous creaking and then release, ice shattering everywhere.

The workshop had begun by the time I got there; the room was warm with bodies, and at the center, the esteemed professor played at a grand piano.

"Dance to the music," he commanded as he played different rhythms, and we swayed on the balls of our feet as the music flowed in the room, and then our arms did too: we were flowers, we were water, we were ice, we were snow.

Such was the music.

One young man was having trouble. He couldn't seem to catch the beat in his body, even though he was known in town as an accomplished musician; he played piano with the most intense emotion, his face crumpling in concentration as he found every note, captured every syncopated phrase meticulously. When he played the piano, his beat was perfect.

But in his body, something had not yet connected.

"Get up," the professor said gently, and moved the accomplished student out onto the wooden floor, and sat himself in front of the piano.

The young man twisted in panic.

"Skip," the professor said softly, "skip for us across the room." He played a soft, lilting air, perfect for skipping—you could feel the music wafting, irresistible.

The student froze. In his body, we read obedience, embarrassment, confusion. Then suddenly he crashed forward, violent as ice sliding off the roof, and skipped in a way that made him look injured, like an animal who'd hurt his leg.

The professor stopped him after a minute, waiting just long enough for him to find a kind of lurching rhythm, more drag-hop than skip. The young man, nearly weeping with relief, stood still in his black-stockinged feet, drenched in sweat and shame…

…and something new. A new understanding of where the music really came from. Not the fingers. Not the notes. Not the metronome.

But the part of the soul that wants to dance. The very core of ourselves.

We all witnessed it that day, this one person coming into awareness, as we all stood in awe and tried to keep our hearts safe in our chests. But we were touched and informed, and there were tears rolling down cheeks as we watched this young man learning to dance to the true beat for the first time. It was a miracle of sorts. And as we witnessed and were a part of this, I realized it was also a convergence. Of all those who had arrived to this day, struggling through snow and ice and weather, in order to be gathered here in a state of awe, in order to witness this event together.

Before you can find the song, you must dance the music. There's rhythm in everything: in the creak of ice crashing from a roof, the burble of water filing a cup, the whoosh of breath in your chest. Today, pay attention in a new way. Listen to the rhythm in everything. This is the sound of the Universe.

34
The energy of loving kindness

A study was done in which it was determined that energy can be broadcast between one person and another, via touch or simply by being in close proximity.[3] Of course, this isn't news to modern energy healers! The belief that energy can be broadcast in this way has long been central to ancient and new age healing modalities. Many of us who work in healing see results so quickly, even instantaneously, that we do not bother with data, outcome, or science.

We see our work as intuitive in nature, not something that requires such rational measurement. And yet, it appears we are beginning to be able to measure exactly this type of energy exchange.

3. Rollin McCraty, Mike Atkinson, Dana Tomasino, and William A. Tiller. "The Electricity of Touch: Detection and Measurement of Cardiac Energy Exchange Between People," *Brain and Value: Is a Biological Science of Values Possible* (1998), via http://www.heartmath.org/research/research-publications/electricity-of-touch.html.

In the study, it was found that there was an exchange of electromagnetic energy produced by the heart when people touched each other or were in close proximity to each other. Interestingly, this exchange was stronger or more resonant when the emotions of loving kindness and caring were expressed between the subjects.

The study did not look at whether there was a signal from a distance—although those who understand and practice energy healing already believe this occurs.

The study also did not address different emotional states, such as what happens to electromagnetic energy when emotions of anger, rage, fear, anxiety and so forth were present.

The study caused consternation from those who didn't want to believe that heart's opening, energy healing or any modalities such as reiki, Matrix Energetics, the Reconnection, the brilliant work of James Nemec or the many other unnamed and unbranded modalities that utilize intention and emotionality to affect change in the body were effective.

These folks most certainly also scoffed at the type of energy work I and others do, in which Divine guides, angels, and etheric medical teams arrive into the room, to work en masse on a person, with results that create emotional healing, soul growth, and even physical healing.

We're all very new to this. Or perhaps we're very old to it. But when science—cold-blooded, "just-the-facts-ma'am" science—starts to notice the energy exchange that happens between people, and to document it

the town square, a small space of perhaps
⁞aming, swarming with these men wearing

⁞otice that one group is wearing blue hats.
⁞s. And the third group, green hats that are
⁞ quite sure which is the dominant theme.
⁞f, or a dance team competition...or some-
⁞pen annually? Or perhaps every day in this

⁞ and laughter bubbles up. A fiddle player
⁞e first group starts their dance, not quite
⁞d lumbering at the beginning, each hold-
⁞ief in either hand—it's an ancient English
⁞unces, once performed deep in the forest
⁞erchiefs wave and flap like white doves.
⁞ something between awe and amusement.
⁞t out good-natured encouragement from
⁞ male chorus and clapping and stomping

⁞know. Some I recognize: "Oh, dear, what
⁞ifferent words, a kind of cheeky, saucy fun.
⁞ng, and I realize we're all part of it, this
⁞uch wild shaking of bells, sudden starts
⁞rweaving of men like a square dance on
⁞erous shouts that punctuate everything

with papers and graphs and numbers, we healers simple smile to ourselves and continue our healing work.

The Divine is energy. You are energy. We have the ability to become Divine at any moment because this is what we are.

———

*Go lay your hands on someone today, and open your heart until it feels like it's
going to burst open. Don't try to heal them or shift them—just put your hands
on them and let the love flow. Keep your hands there until you're done . . . you'll
know when you're ready to move your hands away. Don't worry about mea-
suring electromagnetic energy passing between you. Just enjoy it.*

And then you notice
twenty feet, suddenly str
bells and flowers.

Looking closer, you
One group has on red hat
also flowered—you aren'

Is it a jingle bell playo
thing? Does this event hap
funny little town?

A crowd has gathered
begins a folksy tune, and t
perfectly, with some jerks a
ing a little white handkerch
tradition, a moderator ann
and in the glade. The handl

The crowd watches with
The rival dance teams shou
the sidelines, singing in lusty
to the beat.

Some old songs I don't
can the matter be," but with

The crowd starts laughi
funny jingling dance with m
and stops for effect, the inte
steroids, and the sudden bois

It's one thi
ington, a t
that every
taurant, t
sparkling

It's q
and sud
gle bells

You
pants,
but thi

M

The men are smiling, cheeks rosy with exertion. The men are waving their little white handkerchiefs. The men are laughing and shouting, and the joy bursts out of their chests for all to see.

The Universe works hard to show us exactly what we need, exactly when we need it. On that day, I needed to witness those dancers, waving their handkerchiefs in absolute surrender to the beauty and fun of life. We all did.

———

Be silly. Allow silliness in your life. Open your arms and welcome it! Wave your own white handkerchief in surrender and thanks to all that is fun, amusing, ridiculous, embarrassing, humble, joyful, and playful in your life.

36
The granting of all wishes

The little town of Independence, Oregon (population 7,000), has a wishing well right off Main Street.

Its civic leaders didn't intend to build a wishing well when the park was first built; they thought it was just a fountain. The inhabitants had other plans.

For the first few years, officials posted the fountain with signs that said "Do Not Toss Coins" and "Coins Not Allowed." By now, they've pretty much given up. The vortex is too strong.

On a Sunday morning in late March the fountain burbles pleasantly, coins glinting from the bottom.

It's the kind of day when anything could happen: a drizzle of spring rain, a soft easy breeze, the promise of spring to come.

I don't have a wish to make today... or even a coin to wish upon.

Yet from the corner of my eye I spy a dented old penny lying on the sidewalk a few feet from the fountain, as if dropped in a hurry or lost amid confusion.

I pick it up, close my eyes, and wish that whoever's wish is on this penny…will come true.

I throw the coin in, certain that the Universe is listening…and as I watch the coin fall gently in the water, I feel something in my heart akin to joy.

We're all One, interconnected and infinitely intertwined.

———

Give thanks for the wishes in your life that have been miraculously granted. Consider the idea that someone, somewhere along the line, tossed your coin in the fountain. Now, go help someone else's wish along. Do it anonymously if you like, or directly. Be thankful for all those who have made wishes on your behalf, and now extend the same to another.

37
You are here

Much of the self-help world doesn't address what we really need: what you need, what I need, what anyone needs in our lives. That's because our current state of evolution is so fast that what made sense even a few years ago is no longer current or relevant to where we can go today.

Recently, I was invited to take part in a seminar that promised it would teach me how to access my authentic self. That sounded great! Who doesn't want to live authentically? But as I looked at the list of all the things this seminar promised, all I could think was: I'm already there.

In a nutshell, the seminar promised I would discover:

+ What's holding me back;
+ How to love who I really was;
+ How to live by my own rules; and
+ How to come into full self-expression.

Whew! Now, these all sound wonderful. But at this point in my life, after many years of struggling and stumbling and wandering lost in the desert, I'm not there any more. At this point in my life, like Oprah's column "What I Know for Sure" in her magazine, what I know is this:

Nothing is holding me back. As soon as I feel something limiting me, I look at it and get rid of it; that sometimes takes time, but letting go of limits is an ongoing process, and I am myself fully at all moments—good, bad, ugly. In all ways, I am always myself.

I don't expect perfection. In fact, I'm sure I won't ever achieve it. I'm okay with all my flaws and faults, in addition to my more developed qualities. In fact, even though I am not perfect, I love myself in all ways—full acceptance of all parts of myself. What else can I do?

I already believe my life is my own to create. How could it be otherwise? As an adult living in the time and culture where I live, nobody else is in charge of me but me.

Everything I do is my full self-expression. Again, how could it be otherwise? I fully inhabit myself, and I am a work in progress. This is the same for everyone.

There's this myth that we aren't living who we really are ... when in fact, we are living exactly who we are, every minute of the day.

If we are in fear, we are living fear. If we are in anxiety, we are living anxiety. If we are in shame, we are living shame. If we are in anger, we are living anger.

We are always living exactly the consciousness we have achieved, in that moment. There is no falseness to this.

In addition, we always have the ability to move beyond where we are now—from one stage of authenticity to another.

For example, you can live in shame for decades, and then suddenly just decide it's not your problem, it's not your story, you don't want to live there any more, and in that moment of choice, you break free from that old image or idea of yourself, and suddenly it just all dissipates and dissolves. After a few years, you can't even remember the problems you were dealing with back then.

Your self is always shifting, changing, and moving.

Another way of putting it: wherever you are? You are here.

———

Be thankful for exactly who you are, at this moment. With all your foibles and flaws, all your struggles. Life is a series of experiences that show us the way. At any moment, we can drop our story, drop our old view, and move into a new state. We may do this today, or it may take us years to do this. Whatever you are now is your absolute authentic self in this moment. Be grateful for this experience.

38
Brown-black dog

The first rain of the season is a call for caution where I live. The roads, newly slick with accumulated grease and residue, haven't washed clean since summer. Oil floats on the leaf-strewn asphalt—a shimmer, a rainbow, an iridescence.

And also a treachery.

Around here, we greet the first downpour as a welcome drink of moisture—come fall, everything's gone to chaff and stubble, and we can't wait for the green this will bring. Yet for drivers, the rain is also disorienting.

On an afternoon in early October when I pick up my daughter from middle school, the rain has been falling all day. At 3:15, a patch of blue teases through the skittery clouds, and I ease my way into the lineup of cars in the load-only zone, watching kids pile in with their books and backpacks and science projects.

My daughter, ever attentive, stands at the ready, wearing just a t-shirt and jeans. I've long since given up expecting that teenagers will wear normal things like jackets on rainy days; their bodies run hot, and on days like this—drizzle moving to overcast moving to sun and threatening to circle back again—well, weather is meaningless.

It's just not her reality.

"What's the worse that can happen," she says with a grin. "That I'll get wet?"

She piles into the car with a friend we often drive home, and they chat about the latest teen band, the upcoming dance, and the disgusting food on the school lunch menu. It's all ordinary discussion for an ordinary day.

Yet for some reason, the dread in my heart won't lift.

I drive with excruciating caution in the school zone. The chattering in the back increases in speed and volume and beautiful teenage inanity as I slow further. They're laughing, and I've slowed to 10 mph in a 20, with a herd of impatient cars behind me.

Everything seems normal, everything seems lovely. On my left, I see an older woman is raking leaves in her yard, like somebody out of a Norman Rockwell painting. There are pumpkins on her stoop and the leaves dance in the wind. So beautiful.

Why am I driving so slowly?

The brown-black dog enters my periphery, a flash on my right, for only a second before it's racing across the street toward the woman raking the leaves. The dog bounds forward, a young lab racing across the slick street, oil streaming on the surface.

The friend says loudly and in a strange way, "Look at that dog."

My daughter screams.

I see the dog disappear under the front wheel and I put the brakes on and we slide in slow motion. I wait for the car to hit and I wait for the thud of the dog and I wait for the pain and the grief. I see the dog's owner in the yard to the right, the friendly brick house with the cobweb decorations now frantically pumping her arms up and down on her legs, a hand signal for *no, stop, stay, come.* She is shouting, but I hear no words. The open screen door flaps.

The car skids to a stop. I can't see the dog.

I wait for the thud, the yelp, the squeal.

And then ... the brown-black dog bounds out from the wheel well, a flash in time reversing itself, as if it had never run out at all.

"Did you see that?" I say to the back seat, wanting to make sure I am not the only one who has seen this miracle. My legs are on fire with adrenaline.

"We almost hit that dog," the friend says.

"Did you see that?" My daughter echoes softly.

The sun peeks through the clouds. To my right, the dog's owner is clucking and crying and hanging onto the neck of the brown-black dog.

Sometimes, a miracle happens right in front of our eyes. As if the angels, who have been whispering to us insistently all day to pay attention, slow down, be aware, will also at the last minute reach down and alter the fabric of reality. Change events before they happen. Change events as they happen.

Or sometimes, even after they happen.

————

Angels are here, whether we see them or not. They whisper to us continually, telling us the way in which we should go: to the right, to the left, faster, slower, without hesitation or with caution. They interfere, when interference is necessary. When you look for the reality of a miracle, when you choose to live in the reality of miracles, angels always appear. Close your eyes and think about all the times this has already happened in your life.

Part Six:
Expansion

....

*In which we expand beyond
our selves, and begin to grow.*

39
Speaking our truth

There is a documentary maker I know who's fascinated by the concept of truth.

This man seeks to take off all the costumes, all the camouflage, all the doublespeak that we shout at each other, in order to reveal the truth that lies beneath. The cameras roll, the lights illuminate, his guest relaxes or squirms under his questioning—and the truth comes out.

His goal is to capture truth as it arrives to us—in the moments of vulnerability where we let our armor slip and our true selves are revealed.

He films on location: at people's homes, on the street, in nature, in the city. It all looks so natural. Yet behind the scenes the cameras whir, the beeping green lights blink to indicate the show is live. The clock counts down, the production crew watches on multiple screens, there is editing and cutting later on. All normal parts of a documentary process.

But also—one step removed from the truth as it happens during the show. In other words, by the sheer act of filming, a moment of truth is also a moment manufactured.

I've been on TV a number of times, and each time I have been stunned by the discomfort I experienced in front of the camera. Not because I was being broadcast, or out of concern for my appearance, or because the lights were too hot, or other reasons you'd think. Instead, my discomfort was similar to that of the lost tribes who believed that the camera is a soul stealer. Or at the very least, a truth stealer.

The camera catches us as we struggle to find the truth. It attempts to look inside our soul to reveal the hidden truth within as an absolute, a line in the sand, a definite thing we can count on…and yet most evolving adults don't know the truth.

When we are moving into adulthood, it's easy to state the truth— we are certain where we stand, and who we stand with. But as we get older and we evolve more fully, the truth gets hazy. We understand we're in the process of coming to an uneasy truce with the idea of truth. Or perhaps we're in the process of moving from one truth to another.

As adults, we can no longer baldly state to the camera: this is what I believe. As adults, we have the capacity to believe many things at once; even conflicting beliefs can coexist within us.

Maturity, true adulthood, becomes the process of living without absolute truth. This political party, that religion, this way, that practice … it all doesn't matter too much, as we move forward in our lives.

The facts, the opinions, the dogmas … it all just becomes chatter.

The real truth becomes known to us when we open our hearts and connect with each other and with the pure energy of the Universe, which we call love.

That's about the only real, pin-it-down-and-look-at-it truth that exists.

———

At different stages of your life, you will determine what is true for you. Remember: this is a work in progress. What's true for you last year, two years ago, or twenty years ago may not be true today. Ask yourself if anything in your life is really true. What are those truths? Look deeper, and see if any of these beliefs can be dropped. What are you left with when you ask yourself what is really true for you? Be grateful for this discernment, and your ability to move forward in your life.

40
Age of anxiety

Anxiety can strike at any age, but often it hits us hard when we're first in the process of emerging into our true selves—our adult selves, our authentic selves.

It's a normal reaction of fight or flight, when we have nowhere to run to and nobody to punch.

In other words, anxiety is fear stuck still.

In my early twenties, I worked in downtown Seattle; it wasn't a very big downtown back then, but for me it was big enough: towering office buildings, lots of people, and at that time, a very big homeless population who camped on the streets. To walk anywhere downtown—at least for the young woman I was at the time—meant being accosted, harassed, even assaulted.

It wasn't so much that I was afraid ... although at some level I was. But as I plotted my route from the office to Pike's Place Market where

I often ate lunch, I knew the onslaught was coming. No matter which street I took, at a certain point, I'd need to transverse a certain corridor where I'd be yelled and jeered at, and sometimes even grabbed.

Which is why one Wednesday at 12:20 pm, I found myself deep in the bargain basement of the downtown Woolworth's, a five-and-dime there for many years, not knowing quite how I'd gotten there. I stood surrounded by all kinds of goods and sundries while my heart pounded as if I were having a heart attack, my skin turned clammy, my legs went wobbly, the store shelves loomed before more, and for a moment, I almost passed out.

Panic attack.

When the body can't move into fight or flight, and in modern society, this is often disapproved of … the body nevertheless reacts. All of these physical reactions have no place to go, no place to be released. It's fear stuck still.

We all have our fears … every single one of us. It might be a phobic fear of spiders, a fear of driving over 60 mph, of dark basements, having a check bounce, or the fear of your own non-negotiable, absolutely-gonna-happen-someday death.

Our fears might be rational or ridiculous; it doesn't matter which. But when they get stuck—when they don't have a release through the body—that's when anxiety happens.

It's important to remember that at our core, we are physical beings. We feel things in our body. We collect emotions, thoughts, and other information in our body. If we don't clear our body with exercise, physical exertion, and physical relaxation … that stuff stays stuck.

It is our choice, staying stuck with fear or not. The body never lies. It keeps everything, until we consciously let it go. Yet it is also the most generous to us when we give it time to move, to be free and to release.

———

Close your eyes, breathe deeply, and scan your body with your mind. Scan it from head to toes, from torso to fingers. See what areas call out for your attention. If you have been suffering from anxiety, fear, anger, shame, ask your body where this is located. Allow what your body would like to tell you to come into your mind as a memory, vision, or knowing. Be grateful for this newfound awareness and information, and slowly allow it to be released.

41
Tenacity

When I turned forty, I began writing after a twenty-year gap.

Now, I've been a writer since I was a small child. I wrote through my teens and did major writing in college. When I graduated, I intended to take a year off to write my first novel and ended up instead with a job as an advertising copywriter. I needed the money. It was considered a coup to get this job.

I tucked my short stories and poems and novel starts in a big cardboard box, and in short order entered the world of work, marriage, and motherhood. And pretty soon there wasn't room for writing any more.

If you've ever tread this path, you know already that it's non-stop. You work, you care for kids, you do your best to be in relationship. There is no room for "me time," there is hardly room for "going to the bathroom by yourself" time. It's all lather, rinse, repeat, non-stop every day.

Twenty years went by. And then at forty, something changed.

I would like to say that as I blew out the last candle on my birthday cake it hit me, but it was more subtle than that. There was suddenly a day a few months after I'd hit the milestone when I realized that if I was ever going to live my dream of becoming a published writer, I would have to start.

Now.

Not next month, or even next week. Right now.

I'd need to carve out time and space, and I'd need to bring my whole focus to my intention to write. I'd need to get over my fear of failing at this life's dream. And somehow, I'd need to continue bringing in an income for the family, continue being a wife, mother.

This understanding slammed into me on an ordinary day of picking up kids from school and getting ready to make dinner, and I knew it as absolute.

A few days later, I quit my job. I rented a tiny, terrible office space that was so cold in the winter, I had to wear my down jacket and gloves to type. I showed up every morning to this frosty cell, and worked without break until early afternoon, when it was time to pick up the kids. In the evenings and on weekends I worked freelance jobs to pay the bills.

I did this for one year. And when my shiny bright first novel was done, I packed up a pristine white copy and mailed it off to a New York agency, waiting for the acceptance letter to arrive.

Except, of course, it never came.

I was so naïve, so new to this, that when I did not hear from the agent, I picked up the phone and called them.

"We receive a hundred unsolicited manuscripts a day," a bored receptionist told me. "We just toss 'em."

I could have cried, I could have raged. But instead I educated myself on the publishing industry. I revamped my first novel and got it onto some big agents' desks. Finally, I accepted that first novels don't always get published, and I started my second one.

It is grueling to work for no money, with very little hope, with no program or guidebook to carry you forward. At many times during my second novel I felt like quitting. But I finished, and I sent out queries, one after another.

I sent out thirty queries to agents, and thirty rejections arrived.

But a little voice inside me did not let me stop—and by this time in my life, I'd learned how to pay attention to little voices. "Keep sending them," the voice said. "You will need more than forty." Sure enough, along with my forty-fourth rejection, I also received a very short, very noncommittal email from an agent. "I am intrigued," she wrote. "Please send."

I sent the manuscript. She didn't want it. I was sure my writing career was over.

But a few weeks later out of the blue, she emailed to ask if I'd ever considered writing a nonfiction book. A book about channeling. Would I be interested in talking more?

And of course, this was my first book, *Writing the Divine*.

When we pursue a dream, there are so many times we may want to quit. But sometimes we just need to keep going. The Divine knows the arc of our destiny, our future, better than we do. Stubbornness is not always a fault. If you are passionate about something, move toward it every day. If you have not started yet, begin now.

———

What do you really want to do that you have put off doing? What is your biggest dream, the accomplishment that would please you the most? Consider that you are being invited to step into this reality today. It is your choice, if you would like to begin.

42
Saying yes

We become adult when we step into who we really are.

We don't become perfect or mature, nor do we solve all the problems of the planet—not to mention all of the problems of our personal life, habits, characteristics, and relationships on this earth.

Even when we step into adulthood, we carry our fault and flaws and foibles like coats we've brought along in case of cold weather.

But we do shed one suit of clothing we've been wearing for a long time. Not the innocence of childhood. Not the energy of youth. But the suit of clothing that others have made for us and that we have willingly donned for so many years—the shirt and pants of other people's expectations, other people's desires for us, other people's demands.

The first demands are sewn by our parents, who may want us to be happy, but more often want us to be able to support ourselves, to be stable, to be safe, and to have a job that is well regarded in society as a whole. They are not interested, in the most part, in the path less traveled.

The next demands are those of our relationships, who want us to fit into a way of behaving that serves the relationship. If you are married, for example, your spouse will want you to continue to be married, to do the things that you have always been doing in the marriage. If you are a woman, this might be the cooking, the cleaning, the childbearing, the child caring, the support of the family with a supplementary income. If you are a man, this might be agreeing to go out and make an income that you bring home to support the family. This is a simplistic way of looking at these arrangements, because many modern relationships have more breathing room built in. But many relationships in our society still do not. Often, these are tasks that you have agreed to early, before you know who you are, or who you are going to be.

Finally, society itself puts controls on us; we are encouraged to act a certain way, discouraged from acting other ways. These constraints may be subtle,

In every person's life, there comes a time when these outfits no longer fit. What our parents want for us. What our relationship wants for us. What society wants.

We must walk into the desert, take off all these suits of expectations, and step into who we really are. You may have faced this already, in your own life, and made this rite of passage. You may be getting ready to do this rite of passage soon. You may only see the smallest glimmer of this choice approaching you, a twinkling star in the distant corner of your vision, beckoning you.

People often ask me, "What is my life's path?" or "What is my life's purpose?"

The answer is always: you choose.

If you have always wanted to be a writer, but you find yourself as a banker, then you are not stepping into your authentic self.

If you have always wanted to be a healer, but you are too afraid to take the training required, you are not stepping into your authentic self.

There are always so many reasons to say no, to deny your self, to resist, to be afraid, to stop, to disallow.

True freedom happens when you say yes to who you truly are, and take that path. This is when you step into adulthood, when you take off all the expectations and desires others have for you, and choose your own way, your own pilgrimage of your life.

In my own case, I always wanted to be a writer, but I was not able to start writing until I was forty. I was mothering, working, and simply was too afraid that I would fail.

I finally said yes to my true calling. I walked into the desert alone and began my pilgrimage.

If you are thinking about stepping into your true self today, I say don't wait. Don't wait another moment, another month, another year. If you are afraid, bring your fear along with you. You can jettison it later, when you are further on your path and will know you do not need it.

What do you need to say yes to? Don't say you don't know. You do. Take time today to ask yourself this question over and over again, until you can get to the place where you will answer freely, from your heart's truth. Meditate on this question, pray on it, ask it to be revealed. If you are already walking on your true path, be in gratitude. If you are not yet on your path, be in gratitude for your uniqueness on this planet and for the gifts you have to offer the world.

43
Saying no

One way to become free is by learning to say no.

When we first start out on our path to consciousness, there's this emphasis on yes—we use positive affirmations, we do vision boards, we work with Law of Attraction, the Secret, we hang on to the false belief that intention can only be expressed in positive language—or certain doom will befall us.

To be sure, these first steps of positivity are ways we learn to organize ourselves and our intentions. They're the first tools we use when we're learning to manifest—and to that end, it's all good.

But once we're clear on how to manifest, once we understand how to follow Divine energy, a new challenge will emerge.

We'll have too much abundance—too many choices. And we'll have to learn to choose.

It's almost as if the Universe starts throwing a whole bunch of possibilities our way. Some will be great—exactly what our heart desires! But many will only appear to be what we want—but in fact will only be distractions, temptations, or worse.

It's our job to learn how to discern—how to sort the wheat from the chaff, how to see the diamond from the stone.

Jesus was offered the world by the devil, during his forty days in the desert. During this time, he learned how to step into who he really was by saying yes to the destiny that was before him. He also learned how to say no to what was not his destiny, what was not his true purpose in the world. All the riches, all the treasure, all the power was presented to him, and he denied it all.

I am most certainly not Jesus! But I have found that once I learned the trick of manifesting by saying yes, that the lesson of "no" immediately arrived.

In the beginning, when my work was new and I was unknown, nobody paid me any mind. But later, offers began to trickle in: Did I want to be in this joint venture? Did I want to write for this newsletter? Did I want to travel? Do a book tour? A conference? Opportunities began to arrive—and not all of them were in my best interest.

I did many of these things the first few years. In fact, one year I did 172 events!

This wasn't a good thing—it didn't fit my personality or my deep need for privacy, quiet, and stillness. In fact, I'm not a very good traveler.

I like to keep things really simple in my life. I am happiest at home. This jacked-up schedule made me anxious, tired, and unhappy.

As these things often happened, the more full my schedule became, the more offers came in—many of them having nothing whatsoever to do with anything spiritual or enlightening at all.

After that year of insanity, I took a month off for reflection. During that month I did nothing—I did not write, I did not see many clients, I mostly sat out under the trees, went for walks, and stayed at home. I meditated. I wrote in my journal. I began to relax, to enjoy life again—and I saw how far I'd moved away from my true self by saying yes to everything.

I began to say no to everything that was not truly me, and began to say yes to only what I truly loved: writing, audio, and working with clients.

In a world where everyone seems to want to be richer, more powerful, or more popular, it can be hard to say no. Yet if we are to be our true selves, we must say first yes to all that is us, and no to what we are not.

In discernment, we do not limit ourselves.

In discernment, we become free.

———

What do you need to say no to in your life? What do you need to stop, resist, end or let go of, in order to be your true self? What distractions block you from your true path? Hold these considerations in your mind today. Allow yourself to say "no" to anything that is not your true self, your true path.

44
Stacking stones

The practice of stacking stones is both old and new. In the study of Won Buddhism, for example, ancient stone statues have been shown to have similarities in the configuration, size, number, and geometrics of pagodas constructed long ago.

Even today, people flock to Buddhist temples in Asia and stack stones that represent their wishes, hopes, and petitions, each stone corresponding to an ancestor, family member, or situation in the stacker's life.

You will find these statues not only at Buddhist temples, but worldwide at retreat centers, in gardens and woods and deserts, besides rivers and near the ocean, wherever people might find stones and stack them. Many rock stacks are built simply for luck, the blessings of the gods, or the practice of spiritual devotion.

It's interesting to see that stones are not nature in the same way trees are nature. Stones are not living beings in the normal way we think of sentient forms: having breath, having living.

But the question pulls: do stones have consciousness? Do stones have souls? Spend some time stacking stones in your yard or by a river one long, leisurely afternoon, and you will become to know them more intimately, these creatures that are not creatures, these energy entities that resonate so differently from tree, animal, insect.

In America, even in Europe, we're such young civilizations. In the span of the history of the planet, not even yet a blink of the eye. We don't understand yet how to deal with the big issues of birth, life, death, and the continued, continuous cycle of the soul living in earth body. We're so attached to everything, we suffer all the time. We don't know yet that true spiritual progression takes more than one lifetime.

When we work with stones—these beings or objects that have a much longer history than we do, when we begin to connect with this slower, deeper vibration, we become aware of the vast energies that exist in our world.

To stack stones requires patience. It requires a process of selecting the right stone—the ones that call you for this reason or that. And then fitting these stones in a way so that gravity is precisely courted, balance is achieved. So many things to consider: which stone, how to place it, which stone to place it under or over, and always the intention, whether known or emerging, behind each stone. The totality of the statue as a wish, a prayer, a reminder. For you to see now, and for others to see much later.

Stones are older than we are. They have seen so much, and they remain in place if they are not disturbed. If they are left in peace, they will stand for centuries.

To create a stone statue is to create a statue that stands as a sentinel for the next person, the next beings to discover—even if your stone stack is built privately in a place where only your future self will come across it again.

———

Stack some stones. Notice their heft and weight in your hands. Notice the patience that is required to find balance. Wish some wishes upon your stones or say some prayers. Another time, another day, return to these stones and understand how you and your life have changed. Stones do not change much in a lifetime; we will change enormously. Let the stone stack be a marker for who you are today.

45
Wake-up call

Sometimes we think we want something—but when it arrives to us, we realize that we never wanted it at all.

We just thought we did.

As if there's this gap between what our mind craves, and what resides in the deeper chambers of our heart. What we want in our earth life—and what our soul truly desires.

For years, I'd craved one of those fancy coffee makers—you know the kind. They look like miniature space ships ready to take off from the counter, and they require an elaborate system of add-on purchases to brew: tiny individual capsules of coffee, tea, or cocoa, placed one at a time into the machine. Plunge the lever down and voilà! You've brewed your own personal, private cup.

Talk about instant gratification!

I spent several years drooling over a particular machine in retail shows. I was always first in line when they had them in offices—always the big price tag places, like your mortgage broker, or banker, or your kids' orthodontist.

But for some reason, I always resisted buying one.

It wasn't just the price, although for a coffee maker, I found the price steep.

I didn't think I needed the technology either—I've existed on the single-cup, funnel and filter drip method for decades.

But the real truth is, my idea of absolute luxury is to not make my own coffee, no matter how elegant the machine.

My personal idea of bliss is to have someone bring me a cup of steaming hot coffee, in the particular red or green or yellow mugs that I've used and loved for years, directly to me in bed.

There I am, hair unbrushed, eyes barely open, blanket still snuggly, reaching my arm out for the glorious wake-up cup, and if I am truly blessed that day, whoever is bringing me said cup—partner or one of the teenagers—will sit on the bed and chat with me while I drink it.

Heaven! Nirvana! Bliss!

I think the Universe got tired of me drooling over these machines, when I already had it so good—and they decided to teach me a lesson. Recently I got to stay at a fantastic hotel courtesy of my publisher. I was so excited about the puffy towels, bazillon soft pillows—you could even order a live goldfish for your room in case you got lonely!

But the most impressive to me was they had these special coffee makers, just like I'd always wanted.... pop in the tiny sealed canister, push a button and your brew is ready!

I popped, I pushed, I sipped. I made a cup, and then another cup. And then I made another cup, just for the sheer fun of it.

But the truth was ... sipping coffee in bed, snuggled in the pristine hotel linens, everything fresh and clean and new ... I liked my home coffee better.

The one cup, one cone, one filter method. The sit on the bed and chat method. And I wouldn't trade it for anything.

Sometimes we think we want something, only to find out we don't. In coffee makers ... and in so many other aspects of our life.

The good thing is, the Universe is well aware of what we need; of what will take us to the highest possibility.

––––––

Write a list of everything you think you want. A car, a relationship, a new pair of shoes. A degree, a trip, an experience. Whatever it is for you. Now, ask the Universe to show you if you really want this or not. If this longing, this craving, will actually make you happier and more whole—or not.

Part Seven:
Nature

....

*In which the grace of the
natural world opens our hearts.*

46
Meeting the redwoods

If you live where I do, you've probably done the trip. Snaked down the highway past Eugene, climbed into the mountains, swooped through Grants Pass to Cave Junction. Stopped to gaze in amazement at the herds of elk grazing at the roadside—hundreds of them, less than a hundred feet away, antlers flashing in the sun. Traveled deep into that place where southern Oregon turns to northern California, and everything turns into evergreen and mist.

It's a hard trip to do in winter—it's snowy and rainy and dark—but in the spring or summer, it's magic.

You're heading toward the redwoods. Ancient forest of ancient trees, known for their mystic powers. The excitement builds, for they are not far.

You pass through Humboldt County, where the air is green with marijuana growing in the woods. And faster than you think you've reached Crescent City, where the road opens up before you to a wild blue ocean: a mighty yonder extending out to forever, cresting with the smell of salt and sea. There's a beach…not a nice one. But you get out anyway to stretch your legs and run around, and the seagulls scream above you.

The trees are very near.

The first encounter leaves you devastated. The ranger signs say "redwoods," but these are much smaller trees than you expected. You can tell they're redwood, because of their bark—but size wise, they look just like regular trees. Is this it? Are these the mighty trees you've heard so much about? Two days and a night of travel for this? It doesn't seem worth it.

And yet even as your anxiety builds into a crescendo of disappointment, your car winds farther into the forest, and you begin to notice a change.

It's quieter, suddenly. It's greener. There's a hush in the air. There's a presence. There's something different.

And as you look again at the trees looming past your window, you realize: they are enormous.

It's as if you've moved from the kindergarten playground into the council room for the elders: the granddaddies and grandmamas of the trees.

They are huge. They are aware. They are amazing. They are holy.

You may pull over and get out at this point, parking on a shoulder covered with red bark, and head tentatively into the woods—tentatively, because in the presence of these trees, it is clear that you are in sacred land. Even thirty or twenty feet away from your car you will feel a kind of panic, as if you might never return from this wild, mystical land of trees.

To be in the presence of beings who have been here twice or even three times as long as we have—who've rested in the same spot, absorbing the light and water, simply living as free sentient beings—this is an amazing knowing.

The trees stay with you your whole life. You never forget them, the sacred beings with their rusty red trunks extending high into the sky, their awareness so much beyond ours.

————

This world is filled with places that transport us to states of grace. For me it is the redwoods. Where is it for you? Give thanks now for the places that hold your heart.

47

The Universe is singing

Long ago, I came across a study in which the energy or vibration emitted by sponge molds was found to make a sound that, if magnified a million times, is audible to the human ear. Alas, I no longer recall the source. But the gist of the study was this: These vibrations have been recorded, and what they sound like, these vibrations of sponge molds (arguably lower life forms) are the sounds of whales singing.

It must be imagined that other objects also emit energy. The pillow you sleep on all night with your Beloved's head next to yours. A blanket swaddled around a newborn baby. A flower held in a vase of water.

Perhaps everything sounds like whales singing.

Perhaps everything has its own infinitesimally beautiful and recognizable song, if you are only able to hear it.

Such is the nature of sponge mold. When we understand that sponge mold and whale song, our own hum and whistle in this life are continually playing, a kind of white noise for the soul…we begin to awaken to the idea of the vast and limitless energy of the Universe, and our own intrinsic connection to it.

We aren't just singing. We're part of the song. All of us together, in Divine symphony, each with our own note and tone and rhythm. It isn't just humans in the living chorus, but everything: every rock or tree or company or idea or Universe or whale or sponge mold has parts too. One big, endless, and eternal song.

———

Close your eyes. Listen to everything. Begin to become aware that your very breath, the very way your heart beats in measure at this moment, is a part of the Universal song. You are not separate.

48
Aurora Borealis

Some places you remember for their restaurants, their museums, their cobblestone streets, the way they serve coffee and apéritifs at sidewalk cafes.

I remember Norway for the light. In the winter, the light was elusive. As a kid, we wore reflectors on our jackets, in hopes that drivers might catch the weakest slant of sun, clouded and high, in warning that we were near.

In summer, the light was long and bright and hard—it lasted all day, all night, then past night until it was day again. We stayed up late until we became too giddy with sun; at 11, midnight, or 1 o'clock we pulled down blackout shades, and prayed for sleep the way the elderly do. Elusive, unreachable, a state of being that was not ours those months of summer.

I only saw it a few times, the Aurora Borealis. I was young then, and perhaps I don't remember things clearly. It was fall, or winter by then, and our nights had returned.

We were walking outside, as we often did, and the sky flashed green, and green again, and I felt it was coming from my heart.

They say that these lights are solar particles colliding with atmospheric gases. Perhaps. Or perhaps they are illusion, these northern lights, a sort of mass hysteria brought on by too much sun across an endless summer, the light illuminating our hearts to such a degree that when fall comes, when winter arrives, we can do nothing but emit it back into space, what we have been holding for so long.

Nature is an emotional experience. We hold in our hearts what we see: the sun rising, the sun setting, green lights flashing across the night's sky. Our hearts return this emotion when the experience is long over. Today, watch one: sunrise, sunset, or if you are near the top of the world and the season is right, the Aurora Borealis.

49
The soul sings

A study was done in which every kind of music was plotted and recorded in the most painstaking, precise and esoteric way: the chanting of certain peoples in central Africa, with their intense rhythm and vocal clicks.[4] Birdsong from the Amazon. The songs of Russian immigrants. The dirgy chant of Buddhist monks. The plaintive keen of bagpipes. Hip hop, blues, soul.

When everything had been charted and run through a computer, when everything had been digitized and analyzed and made into binary combinations and bar charts and graphed in every kind of way,

---

4. Victor A. Graer. "*Some Notable Features of Pygmy and Bushmen Polyphonic Practice, with Special Reference to Vocal Polyphony in Europe.*" The Proceedings of the Fourth International Symposium on Traditional Polyphony, 2008, via: http://www.polyphony.ge/uploads/fortheng/09_grauer_eng.pdf

and played backwards for good measure to see if Paul was really dead, what was found was this:

The African music graphed the same as the Russian folksong, which graphed the same as the birdsong, which graphed like soul, which matched African drumming which matched exactly the breath call of didgeridoo.

In all music, there were Universal constants, a synchronicity too close to be random.

In the study, they showed examples of this. It was true: all music was the same. They presented their notations; they referred to their data. But in the end, the explanation given was not scientific.

It is because we hear the same music in our soul, the researcher said.

Our souls sing the same music.

———

Go to a live music performance. This may be a concert, a symphony, a street musician, yourself playing piano, yourself singing in the shower, or your child singing a song. Listen past the words and notes to the Universal song underneath.

Today, sing aloud, hum, or whistle, as often as you can. Notice how this activity causes joy and gratitude to swell to bursting in your heart. Notice how you are smiling when you are singing.

50
The magical variety

I learn from trees when I can, the magical variety that exists: maple, oak, madrona, yew, pine, fir—so many more, depending on where you live on the planet.

Each known by the shape and suppleness of its skin, by height and breadth, by color and variegation and curl, by the way each vein grows. Each fully its own.

It is the same with this world: one person is Caucasian, another Chinese, some are young, others old. We separate into our specifics. We even wave differently in the breeze, some of us supple and springy in response to wind, time, the forces of life.

Others of us stand heavy, proud totems, lichen our parasites, ferns our cannibals, our very existence rooted upon the ancestors that rot beneath our roots; our own progeny will use us as fodder in which to sprout, root, naturalize.

There is no time that we exist independent from ancestor or descendent, no time we are fully on our own. We are always as a part of what has been, as a part of what to come. This is frightening to some.

But it is just the way.

When you are out among the trees today, whether you are in the forest, a park or even in the city, look at the uniqueness of the species you find. Now, look at the uniqueness of the people you see. All of us so different, yet all of us the same.

Living beings. Sentient beings. We breathe of the same air.

———

If you are able to plant a tree today, do so. If you are able to see a tree clearly, looking at the veins in a leaf, or the budding cone of a conifer, do so. If you are able, walk amongst the trees, listening to their whisper. They will bring peace to your heart.

51
The love of animals

Late this summer, I had an extraordinary experience with a dog.

It was hot that day, the kind of hot where the grass has dried into stubble and crunch, and the trees have their tongues hanging out; leaves dry and brittle.

I'd headed to a friend's house to work on a project, and when I got out of the car and walked to the door, both of her dogs, gorgeous Siberian Huskies, one all white, one mostly white, were standing behind a baby gate with their tongues hanging out like leaves.

I was wary as I approached the door: I love dogs, but you need to respect 'em. I moved slowly and softly, ready to be barked at. Suddenly, the strangest thing happened. The dog on the right, the dog with the pure white coat and blue eyes pale as the sky began to smile at me.

Smile.

I could actually see the twinkle in his eyes, and his mouth stretched in a grin.

"You're smiling at me!" I said in amazement to him, and his grin stretched wider.

I was still moving slowly, I was still careful. These dogs didn't know me, and they were big. I clambered carefully over the baby gate and into the dining room where my friend was working.

They made way, easy and mellow.

When suddenly, as I walked in fully present, this white dog with sky eyes came over to me and very slowly, very gently, stood up on his hind legs and put his paws on my shoulders: one on the right, on the left.

He stood there for a moment—a minute, two minutes—and I stood there too, staring into his face. And after a moment, I realized what was happening.

He was hugging me.

I connected into his soul, as I often do with animals, speaking soul to soul rather than in language, and thanked him. All was well. He was honoring me.

I honored him back.

The rest of the afternoon as we worked at my friend's dining room table, he lay under the table, right at my feet. Several hours went by, but he stayed right there.

Peace pervaded the room.

———

All animals are sentient beings. We can speak to their souls if we choose ... We can speak to their souls whenever we remember. Try to communicate today with an animal you do not know. Feel the peace that comes from connecting with animals.

52
Crossing the stream

We're at Kah-Nee-Ta. A warm spring, a casino, a resort, a campground in eastern Oregon. People come here for all reasons; those are just four.

We're here for a few days, my partner for a conference, me to do some writing. We've driven 140 miles to get here, traversing the state as trees give way to scrub give way to desert and I realize we have reached a new land, a new sense of place.

I've never been anywhere like this, but I am getting used to that.

The more I travel, the more I realize how big the world is, and how many places there are, and how there is no way I will visit them all, or even most of them, or even a few, before I die.

This particular place, established in 1855, was once owned by a shaman, a spiritual teacher who used the natural plants and roots for ceremony and medicine.

The casino doesn't match the historical vibe; we're numbed by the noise and light, the sour smell of cigarettes as we pass through. That's not what we're here for.

We swim in the giant pool at the center of the resort. It's nice, a luxury for early autumn—but that's not what we're here for, either.

Pulled by some unknown cosmic string to the experience that will be our destiny in this new place, this place we have never set foot in before, we decide to head toward the small town down the road. Sure enough, as we merge onto a main road bordered by nothing but rock and sand and sage, the sign appears: "Horses for Rent."

It's a tiny place, hardly a place at all. There are no horses, just an empty stable and rickety old trailer serving as a front office. There's nobody in the trailer either, just an old paper coffee cup on the floor, and some newspaper inserts and a fly buzzing around to stay warm. We're disappointed, and made a little nervous by the desolation we've stumbled upon.

"Hey," a young guy yells at us from out of nowhere. He's very small, muscled, brown, with a thick black plait of hair down his back. I don't know where he came from.

"Hey," he turns and yells at something behind him, and a mini stampede of horses barrels toward us: a rider and horse leading three more horses, all galloping full force at us. The rider whirls and stops. Same black hair, same brown skin. A girl.

We decide, to my amazement, that we'll take the four-hour half-day's ride with these two young people we have just met. We will take the four-hour half day's ride up high into the hills, these mountains of tumbleweed and slippery sand, even though I have only ridden a horse a few times in my life, and our guides, we find out later, are ages sixteen and eighteen.

The mountains loom. The sky is gloaming. The sweet sage fills the air and the old saddle creaks as I throw my leg up like a cowboy, get stuck, have to try three times while everyone laughs and finally the boy who's just sixteen has to boost me up by the butt into the saddle.

My whole body is trembling as we set off on our journey. My horse, wise soul, knows I am terrified and cares not a whit. I grasp my water bottle with one hand, my saddle horn with the other, and pray.

The funny thing about fear is, once you hang out there for a while, it goes away. We pick our way among rocks, and I marvel that my horse can move all four legs so easily. We veer off toward more rocks, then descend into a slanting riverbed, and finally a stream. It's a trickly stream a first, only a few inches deep. It's fun, and I'm laughing and crowing with delight—the river burbling bright, this clear cold day, the mountains rising.

We travel further, and the water gets deeper. Our guides, unconcerned, press on. The water is now at my horse's chest, and in a turmoil of panic I don't know whether to jump off and lead my horse, or jump off and splash back to shallower waters. Our guides, ahead of us, are talking quietly to each other. The thought of trying to get back on my horse again keeps me glued to my saddle.

But now my horse is chest deep in the water, which suddenly has become dark and cold and whirling. I am clinging to my saddle ready to call out in panic, when our guides begin a kind of clicking and calling and coaxing on cue, and suddenly our horses are lunging across the river, swimming strong across the ripply, dark, cold water, and before I can do another thing, we are lumbering up the river bank, to the other side.

My legs are wet, my shoes sodden. I do not say a word. We spend the rest of the four-hour half-day trip climbing high into the mountains, and I am still so amazed I have forded a river on the back of a horse that my heart does not stop thumping and my eyes do not stop shining until later in the day when we finally arrive home.

I tuck a rock in my pocket and some sage to remember this day.

But I don't remember it until many years later, when I am thinking about miracles, and experiences and life in the world, and all the times my heart has burst open.

———

We each have had unexpected adventures in our lives. Think back to an event in which you stretched yourself or were stretched. Remember this day, what happened, and how amazing you felt. Take this memory out like a precious jewel, and hold it in your hand.

53
Breathing light

Trees talk. Perhaps you have heard them?

Even now, I can't always understand their words. Nevertheless, they whisper to us of life, of what they know, the older ones especially, those who have stood rooted to their spot for 70, 100, 200 years, holding that same ground, watching life change around them in the smallest, most private way: the sudden unfurling of a new leaf that did not exist the day before, its sudden, unexpected emergence into full flower of green.

Trees share space with lichen, birds, moss, snails, ants, small bugs, chameleons, ivy, ferns. This is just what I see. In other places, there may be other things. Small animals nest in them, and larger one make them their homes. These beings all scurry, procreate, live, die. Trees see it all, every second, even when it is dark and they pretend to be sleeping.

They are awake at every moment.

Trees are vertical beings, striving, reaching, unfurling to touch the sky, perhaps because they know we believe God lives in the ether.

Yet trees are also horizontal creatures, replete with so much surface area, their branches spread like arms opened for embrace, each leaf a tiny hand reaching, grasping, opening, yearning for light.

In. Out. Branches rustle and sway.

In. Out. Leaves shiver.

In. Out. They are breathing light.

———

Imagine yourself breathing light. Picture every cell in your skin like a leaf straining to the sun. Think tree thoughts! And, as an experiment, go sit quietly in nature, rooted to one spot for a longer than you think you can. What if you lived your whole life in one spot? How would this stillness, this rootedness change you?

Now, think of yourself as a tree; what kind would you be? What would this life look like—to be still and rooted? Make a list of all the ways you are still, all the ways you are rooted.

54
The music of sunset

You hear it before you see it.

Hidden in the tall grasses, the frogs begin their collective croak. The wind rises in accompaniment, rustling in the trees. And the birds! They break out in solos worthy of a stint on Broadway, each out-calling the other in trips and trails of song.

Day is done. The sun is setting.

They know before we do.

But oddly, on this perfect late summer day, when the sun is just setting across the mountains; even now it's falling, falling, falling so quickly you can only count a second or two.

One one-thousand, two one-thousand.

Even now, the moment you notice the light is beginning to change, the moment you look to see the sun is setting, you notice it is setting farther to the left than it was the day before.

You have not moved. The planet has.

The frogs croak a melodic, hushed mantra in steady beat with each other.

It is so rhythmic, you forget to hear it, until it's all you can hear. The sun sets, and you forget to notice, until it's sinking so quickly you catch your breath until it disappears.

One one-thousand. Two one-thousand.

The most beautiful things in life happen so quickly.

A second, two seconds is sometimes as much time as we have to look up, open our eyes, and notice the beauty that is around us.

It is the gift of a summer's night—the sun sinking down into the mountains like lovers folding into embrace.

It is a gift for you, if you are there for the noticing. Breathing. Listening. Watching with your full heart, not just your eyes.

———

Ten minutes before sundown, go outside, face west, and pay attention to what happens. Use all your senses: sound, smell, taste, the feel of the pounding of your heart in your chest, the way your feet stand firm on the ground. Winter, spring, summer, fall; there are miracles in these moments when day changes to night. Let yourself witness these with thanks.

Part Eight:
Awareness

....

In which we begin to transition into our true selves as Divine beings.

55
Lock into the hum

There are times in a church service, in any church or denomination, at any feast or holiday or prayer service, even in any gathering, when the energy in the room becomes palpable.

I experience this as a "hum."

At a certain point in the many Catholic ceremonies, for example, there is a time when the congregation joins hands, one to another, each to the next, and recites the Lord's Prayer aloud together. Other religions have other traditions.

It is interesting to watch the discomfort of people who don't know each other suddenly reaching across the room, across the pew or chairs or space between them to join hands. It is interesting to watch the initial uneasiness, the halting shyness, the breaking open of hearts, when people who don't like each other, or family members who have been arguing, suddenly reach to hold each other's hand, and the mood in the room suddenly changes.

At this time, at this tipping point of energy in which there is consciousness in the collective, if you look carefully, you will see a thickening of the air, a golden paleness of light that suddenly suffuses everything.

If you notice carefully, and listen with not just your ears but your entire soul, you can lock in. Lock into the humming, vibrating energy that has somehow become alive in this space.

Perhaps this is why churches, cathedrals, temples so often have such tall ceilings. To allow more room for the energy to rise. So those who are there can feel it, can see it. So those who are there can lock into the hum, when we are together as souls.

―――――

Spiritual celebration in community has been a part of the human experience for thousands of years. When we come together, the Universe is there with us too.

What does locking into the hum mean to you? Where do you hear or find the "hum" in your life? Look and listen carefully today. The hum of the Universe is always there when you pay attention.

56

A single drop of water

With the spring comes the rain, at least here in Oregon. The deluge begins in late October and doesn't stop until March; we wake up to the drip, drip, dripping and then sit huddled in our dark houses as water falls and fills and eventually floods; so much so that the creek overflows, so much that in some years, the city streets are impassable.

This does not happen every year, but this year it did.

One of the unfortunate casualties was a neighborhood soccer field, built decades ago in the unfortunate likeness of a shallow bathtub— the field lower than the surrounding hillocks.

By the first day, the grass was saturated. By the second day, the field was capped by a glistening sheet of water. By the end of five days, as the mid-afternoon sun weakly glimmered through the scudding clouds, the water had risen so high it no longer seemed like a good idea to wade onto the field; it was three feet deep in places, and neighbors brought out canoes and kayaks, paddling between the soccer goal posts for the sheer audacity of it.

But the water was not to be underestimated. Even in this calm before the storm, we all could see that.

By day six, the city officials were swarming in a panic, zipped up in their Gore-Tex and ordering sandbags and the evacuation of the local school a few blocks away. The dam was about to burst, so to speak: a quarter inch more of water, and this field, this giant bathtub filled with hundreds of thousands of gallons of water, this small lake where there had been no lake before, was about to overflow.

Would it happen? When? How much water could the bathtub/field hold?

We watched in suspense as a lone kayaker paddled from the goal line to midfield, the rain pouring down in torrents upon us all.

Sometimes, there's a point where one drop of water is all it takes. One single raindrop that floods the equation and unleashes a powerful force.

We don't know where this one drop of water is before it splatters into reality and changes everything. We can see it forming in the gray clouds above, darkening their silver rims with moisture. We can see it in the energy of those witnessing its arrival: their grim faces, anxious looks.

At times in life, there's always going to be that one single raindrop, that one single drop of water that falls into a place that is already out of balance, and causes the release of everything.

The Universe seeks balance. One way or another.

In this case, the dam did not burst on this particular field. It released somewhere farther south, when the creek rose into the first floors of many homes and businesses along its banks. The resulting torrent of water and mud and debris somehow alleviated the field's great need to flood. It just sat there, filled to brimming yet not brimming.

The water raged along the streets, the water raged in buildings, but the field held its own.

Next time, it seemed to say.

Another time, perhaps.

The rest of the week carried out as these things usually do. The Red Cross came in. Funds were raised. Repairs were made. Water was mucked. The field, now a soggy, dirty mess of mud and grass, absorbed itself.

We forgot about it quickly enough, as we always do.

It wasn't until one day this spring that I notice a peewee team playing on the field, resplendent in their bright uniforms and bright faces.

"Shoot it," one kid called out, and his teammate sailed the ball through the goal posts, blissfully unaware of the kayakers who'd been there just months before.

———

Things change. The rains eventually stop. The rains eventually begin again. Understanding that change is a way to detach from anxiety, fear, panic. If you understood that bad times would be followed by good would be followed by bad, and so on, how would this allow you to relax into your life with gratitude?

57
The secret life of plants

Studies of flowers and plants have been done which show that when one plant in a room is dying, when it is under stress from lack of water, too much sun, placement too near a heater...the other plants in the room will send energy.

This is the best and only way to describe it. The other plants send energy, so that a plant kept alone in a jar without water of any kind, when placed in a room with other plants, will still retain its vibrancy and life.

Photos have been taken of this phenomenon: plants sending energy to each other.

In other studies, when a person in the room is crying—a baby or someone overcome with grief—plants will emit a similar energy.

It is perceived as the look of light: a warbled coloring, like an oil spill, like a rainbow of colors, all the spectrums sliding atop each other. Hazy and evanescent, like an aura.

Such is the nature of plants, flowers, trees: vibrant, empathetic, symbiotic. Humans. Animals.

We are not the only sentient beings.

————

Do you have a green thumb? Do you sing to your plants? Do you talk to the trees, converse with the flowers? Consider today, that plants are also sentient beings. This includes big plants, such as redwoods; prickly plants, such as cactus; tiny weeds sprouting from a crack in the sidewalk. Today, be in gratitude for plants of all kinds. Thank them for their part in your experience.

58
The air is not empty

It mists in through the open windows, creeps in through the open doors; and permeates the breeze until we can't get it out of our noses, our hair, our skin.

It's an early September evening in Oregon, and the scent of mint fills the air.

"Toothpaste," my younger daughter remarks.

"Mint ice cream," my son counters.

"Mojitos," my older daughter proclaims.

The scent is overwhelming; it's as if we'd crushed bowls of mint on the kitchen counter.

Yet it arrives to us from miles away, borne over fields far across the river where acres and acres of mint have been harvested these past days.

Living out here, we're used to the air and what it brings:

Some day soon, the air will hold the smoky, cedar smell of wood stoves burning.

When winter comes, we'll awaken to the clean, cold scent of snow, and we'll look out to find the fields covered in white.

When the year has turned and it is spring again, the pollen will inhabit the air so thick and cottony, it will burn our noses. Our eyes will weep with it.

We often say there is nothing to the air; that it is just air, empty space.

Yet in truth, all air contains particulate: mint, smoke, snow, pollen.

Even in what we call empty space, there is simply more empty space.

Just as we can perceive infinite expansion—a Universe without end—we can also perceive infinite contraction.

We become aware of the air because of what it contains. It is not empty when it is wafting mint; it's not empty, ever.

————

The air around us contains all the complexities of energy and infinite expansion of everything in the Universe. Don't misjudge it or ignore it; instead, give thanks. It brings you messages, joy, beauty, vibration. It is as full as anything else in the world.

59
Three Buddhas

Three Buddhas sit on my desk, arranged in a view I find most pleasing. The medium-sized one sits in lotus on the left. The thicker, burly one sits in the middle. The thin one settles on my right. Each is hand carved of teak, carefully burnished to a rich, reddish bronze, so that the light catches their features: the shape of their three noses, the way their eyelids close in meditation, the drape of their robe and the way their hands are clasped in mudra.

I came across the Buddhas at a small gift store in Kaua'i adjacent to an old stone church: Christ Memorial Christian. The cemetery beside the church has gravesites dating back more than a hundred years, and many of the headstones, carved in lava rock, have since disintegrated so badly that they are unreadable, a pile of porous stone threatening to crumble at any moment.

Young palm trees scatter throughout the cemetery, new beings rising from the old. The sun is hot and strong. And down the road the Kilauea Bakery is putting out new muffins alongside the tiny scattering of shops, in which my Buddhas were found.

My Buddhas, medium, thick, and thin, did not come from Hawaii. They were imported from Bali, where on one day not too long ago, someone carved them by hand, one after another. Each is unique, and I imagine the carver sitting on a straw mat with a straw hat to shade him from the sun, carving the faces of people he already knew. Friends. Family. Those who had gone before.

I think this, because each of my Buddhas is so unique: the one with medium body has a flat, wide nose and a generous mouth. The one that is thick and sturdy has a big nose, long face, enormous ears. The one that is thin has a thin nose, large almond eyes, and a thin mouth.

I imagine the carver laughing as he shows his friends and family members his creations: "Look, this Buddha is you," he says to his high school buddy. "Look, this Buddha is you," he says to his mom. "Look, this Buddha is Grandpa," he tells his family, as they all remember their departed ancestor with pleasure.

He carves the faces of his friends and family into Buddhas and then sends them to a different country, where an unknown person will place them on her desk and look at them each day as she is writing.

Even as I type this sentence, I am looking at the faces of someone's friends or loved ones. I am looking at the faces of Buddha. I realize that Buddha is the face of everyone, with every kind of eyes and nose and mouth and ear shape. Everyone is Buddha, all of us.

————

Buddha. Jesus. God/One/All/Divine. This is all around you. This is also you. And this is in every person you will come across today. Know this, as you greet this person, interact. Know this as you argue and disagree. Know this as you hold compassion, and as you love. All Buddha, all the time, with many, many faces.

60

In the moment of noticing

On a warm Sunday in early spring, I sat in the audience for a dance performance.

The company, hailed as one of the bright lights in the international dance community, was premiering several dances to an "intimate" audience in Portland, Oregon. About sixty of us sat in creaky folding chairs along the back of the rehearsal space while the dancers danced without lights or curtain, with minimal props and costumes, directly in front of us.

"Intimate" is the correct word, for it is something to have a front row seat at a performance this small. The dancers' anxieties, their desire to please become your own. Droplets of their sweat flick on you. Their breath, ragged with effort, commingles with your own, and with the breath of everyone in the room.

The miracle of the body in motion, the rapt attention of the audience, the light streaming through windows, the unexpected creativity of the choreography—all contributed to a spellbinding performance for the first hour…

And then, something changed.

During the second half of the performance, I began to grow restless, as if I could only view so much amazing, breathtaking beauty. I could feel the audience shifting with me. There was a groaning of the flimsy folding chairs, as collective mind wandered.

The dancers, even with all their focus, also sensed it: they were young, nineteen- and twenty-year-olds, and the energy they had expended was no longer in reserve. One dancer was breathing heavily in a way that made us all uneasy. Another dancer looked angry, pressing her hands against her hot cheeks as if to keep from crying.

Our spell, our mutual transfixion, had somehow been broken. We sat uncomfortably, waiting for what was next, as the music swelled in crescendo across the room, then drifted into uneasy silence.

And then, in that moment, the miracle came.

For even while the dancers danced courageously, a large black bee, much bigger than normal, a blimp of a bee, a dirigible, an inch long at minimum, suddenly wandered in through an open window, and began a slow, buzzing parade directly across the stage.

It did not fly quickly, or angrily, or with any sense of purpose. It simply meandered, a zigzag of presence across the stage, through the dancers, into the dance and finally across the room, where it exited, stage right, through the distant open window.

The audience sat, mesmerized. The dancers, momentarily out of dance, allowed the bee to pass. The bee, regal as anything, simply moved through the room, as if none of us were there at all.

When it was done, we could not stop ourselves from applauding.

Life can be like this. There's so much stimulus, so much to look at, we lose our ability to pay attention. Then something happens, and we are snapped back into present moment, amazed at what we have witnessed.

———

The most unexpected events can bring us together. Look in your own life today, and notice what happens that is unexpected, a surprise. How does this affect you, change your mood, or remind you of something today?

61
Out of body

It happened for me first at Krishna Das. One minute you're there chanting a kirtan in a room full of strangers who are progressively opening their hearts until it's suddenly one big heart overflowing and nobody is a stranger any more. The next you're down and out for the count, in full trance—and possibly more.

Kirtan, basically, is call and response chanting. The leader sits on a stage and sings a mantra, a series of chanted words often in Sanskrit. The words themselves are said to be the names of God/One/All/Divine. They're also easy to sing, easy to remember, and easy to follow. The leader sings out the first line of chant, the crowd sitting in the audience repeats it, and this goes on, for twenty minutes, an hour, several hours on end.

What happens is what always happens whenever you go into any kind of trance: when you're driving, or taking a shower and the shampoo lathers up and you can't remember what you're doing and stay in there for way too long. When you're walking in the woods, noticing the trees and birds and everything. When you're running and suddenly time goes away, or lifts, or stands still. When you're listening to healing music with headphones on, or repeating the rosary forty times or meditating on something a hundred and eight times. What happens is that your brain goes into trance, sometimes light, sometimes deeper, and your bouncing, wild monkey mind suddenly has no thoughts to hang on to—they're hanging on to the repetitive mantra instead.

And thus, the thoughts, the brain, the mind itself is finally able to relax.

And in this state of relaxation, consciousness is reached.

I'd never been to a kirtan before Krishna Das—it was held at a big Unitarian church in downtown Portland, Oregon, the weather wet and gray. The sanctuary was stuffed with people wearing various forms of jackets and Gore-Tex and wet weather gear, as is common in these parts. Soon the jackets came off, and were stuffed under the pews or made space for on the floor near the front of the sanctuary, and Krishna Das took the stage.

He's an ordinary looking guy, born and raised in New York, who first traveled to India as a young man, and came back changed.

The first chants were easy, but it soon got more complex. Basically, Krishna Das sings. And then you, the group, the community, the *satsang*, sing it back to him. After about ten minutes, I felt the panic rising, sure I would be unable to follow. I looked around for printed sheets of the lyrics, the way you might consult the hymn book at a Christian church, but there were none. I heard the voices around me, to the left, to the right and to the back, and I realized nobody else was doing much better, either. But together as a collective, the change came out with strong energy.

What happened next was unexpected. About twenty minutes into it, I was on top of the kirtan—I was chanting correctly, my voice in key, fully focused on the mantra and the rhythm, starting to have fantasies that Krishna Das would hear my voice, me in the third row, seventeenth from the left, and stop everything and ask me to please come up on stage and sing backup for him...when I suddenly slumped over in my seat.

The chant roared all around me, energy streaming and coursing through the room and I was out of it, snapped into hypnotic trance by the force of the repetition and the music; and at the same time, slumped over in my seat, I was magnificently aware in a way I had not experienced before.

People talk about out of body experiences—about rising from their bodies, so that they are no longer in their bodies but hanging out on the ceiling, or even blasting out into space where they can look down at their body doing whatever it's doing.

This was what happened to me. At this point in the kirtan, my body remained where it was in the chair, while my consciousness rose to the rafters, and it hung out there in the energy and vibe and air for how long, I do not know.

At some point I felt my earth self, my small silly self, my tiny consciousness nudging me. "Help, I'm stuck," it whispered, and although I tried to call my rafter self back into my body, it would not return. "Help me," I heard again.

I became quite nervous, internally agitated. My consciousness was quite happy floating round the ceiling with all the other spirits and energy there—but what if I couldn't come back into my body?

At this moment, my partner noticed that I had been slumped over for a while and gently touched me on the knee, and then placed his hand there more fully. This is all the reminder I needed.

My consciousness flew back in like Peter Pan reattaching his shadow. It swooped down from the ceiling and found its way home, and my eyes flew open, and I was back in my body, back in the room, back at the kirtan, and Krishna Das was still singing away up on stage and he had most definitely not asked me to be his backup singer.

I noticed suddenly what he's wearing: a red t-shirt, a really old shirt. It's like I've never seen a red shirt before, and as I looked around the room, everything came into my eyes in a new way: it was brighter, warmer, richer.

I reached for my partner's hand and eased back in the humanity of my body.

At that time, I was at the beginning of many consciousness expansions in my lifetime, and I did not know it yet, but it would be an amazing journey.

When have you gone out of body? When have you gone so deeply in trance that you could not get out? If you have not had these experiences yet, consider having them today. Listen to www.mantraradio.co; buy CDs by Krishna Das, Jai Uttal, Wah! Listen to ambient music while lying on the sofa with headphones on. Dance in your own way for as a long as you like. Enter trance, relax your brain, connect to Divine consciousness. When you are done, come back to your body and give thanks for how bright your earth life suddenly is.

62

Abundance is always present

The road I drive each day cuts through an ancient apple orchard, curving and winding through farmland which has long been let go.

It's mostly overgrown now: the once orderly orchards are now a tangle of meadow and new forest. But there are still old apple trees amidst unkempt land—gnarled with age, and growing so close to the road it's almost dangerous.

During the height of the harvest, they scatter their abundance upon the road; golden yellow apples, small enough to fit in the palm of your hand, drop onto the road, not just one, but hundreds.

And then, these same apples stay on the road for weeks; ripening until their skin splits from the sun, sweetening until the point of rotting. The animals come and partake, then the birds and insects. But mostly, the apples just lie there until they're run over by cars and finally washed away by the autumn rains.

A few times, I've seen intrepid folks with apple baskets: light-weight wooden containers that they carry around their necks while they pick. They'll be out there for a few hours, picking baskets full.

And yet mostly, the apples go to waste.

After all, it's not an orchard any more—it's a road through an orchard. It's almost as if we can't see the apples outside of our understanding of "orchard." It's almost as if apples don't exist for us when we see them out of context.

And yet—here is magnificent abundance: bushels of apples that fall to the ground, then are smashed under car tires as people drive to work, school, wherever they're headed on a busy morning, windows rolled up against the crisp fall air, minds busy with a million thoughts, oblivious to what is actually around them.

These apples roll onto the very path that we travel. And yet only a few will even notice them. Fewer still will harvest this abundance.

I stopped the car one misty morning, pulling to the side of the road as commuting drivers swerved past me. I looked up into the branches of this tree still laden with apples, and smelled their apple smell, and listened to the slow hum of bees droning across the ground, glutted with sweetness.

And then, after I'd had my own fill of this perfect morning, these perfect unclaimed apples, the very sweetness of the bees underfoot … I got back in my car, and headed on my way. The apples are probably still there, for whoever will slow down enough to see them.

So often we think the gifts aren't there, because we can't see the orchard for the road. But if we will only slow down, and allow ourselves to relax into Divine view, the abundance is there—within easy view, within simple grasp.

———

Today, drive a new route. Look with new eyes. Take your mind off your thoughts and simply see what is in front of you. Be thankful as you notice the gifts you may have missed before when you were too busy searching. When we become present, abundance is everywhere.

63
Holding space

When I'm teaching a group of folks how to connect with their guides and angels, I'll take them through a special meditation that makes this possible. It's an intensive process, filled with understanding, heart opening, healing and other miracles, and when it's over and I bring the group back to everyday reality, people are usually pretty zoned out for a while.

They look stunned. They can't speak coherently. They're unable to follow a discussion. They can't take in more information.

Many cry, or have to collect themselves.

At this point, before anybody can talk or process or think about things too much, I like to switch gears—and anchor the experience even in the body.

I have everybody get up, stretch, and start milling around the room until they "randomly" cluster in small groups of four. Then, I'll ask each person to take up a specific position: one person to act as receiver, the other three as Divine guides. The receiver stands in the middle, and each of the guides takes up position to the left, behind, to the right, just as the guides arrived in meditation. Every person in a cluster will keep switching positions, until each has had a chance to experience every position.

In essence, we are "modeling" or holding space for ourselves as a receiver, and also as a guide. And what begins to happen in the room when this takes place is more miracles.

A man with a red shirt stands in the middle of one cluster with his eyes closed; he is the receiver. To his left, another man stands silent, gazing at him with the pure love of a guide. Behind him, a woman holds space as another guide, arms open with energy. To the right, another woman also holds space, eyes closed, swaying softly.

In another cluster, a woman is at the center. She is crying softly, with her hands on her heart. To the left, behind and to the right of her, women in the positions of guides are holding their hands up in comfort, radiating pure love and healing.

In other clusters around the room, the energy is sacred, devout, amazing—and I stand in awe, facilitating, watching as this connection of hearts and souls takes place.

The energy in the room is crackling; I can see flashes of light bouncing off the man's red shirt, the auras of all four people in his group expanding and blending into one glow of light. The love in the air is beyond understanding—and to my shock, I notice that the space behind me is filled with guides and angels who've come to watch—the Divine audience forming, yet again.

Each person in every cluster is emitting the kind of pure love that the guides and angels have for us at all times: the true delight that they take in us as we are now; the true compassion that they hold for us at all times.

The exercise goes on in the room for many minutes, as each person takes a turn at being the receiver, as each person takes a turn at being a guide. The vibration rises and rises until I notice that most people have elevated into pure bliss: we can't stop smiling, we can't stop laughing, our hearts are open so big, they are literally filling the room as one heart. Even the people who are crying start laughing, gazing around this room filled with joy.

We get so busy in our lives, so distracted, we forget how easy it is to connect in with Divine entities and energies, and with the Divine in ourselves.

And yet, when we hold space as Divine, whether in a workshop activity or whenever we helping another, we realize the true reality of our existence—that the aspect of pure consciousness, pure love, resides in each of us.

We are not pretending when we hold space.

We can hold space for this, because it is what we are: Divine holding space for Divine.

———

It's one thing to know it in the mind. It's another thing to feel it in the body, with full open heart—this understanding that guides, angels, entities of light and love are always here. This is the true reality, the Divine nature of our experience.

Today, pay attention to the energies around you. Understand with gratitude that there are guides and angels with you at all times, and begin to understand the many layers and levels of consciousness that are true Divine reality.

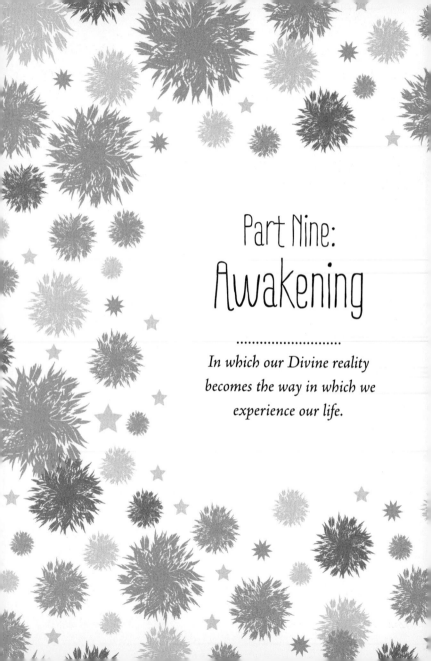

Part Nine:
Awakening

....

In which our Divine reality
becomes the way in which we
experience our life.

64
Electrons, consciousness, soul

There was a time in elementary school when we learned what electrons were. Like angry bees, I imagined them—busy, buzzing bits of energy, always pinging around the room in constant confusion.

I would like to suggest that we are like electrons.

We run from here to there, chaotic blurs of busyness, and even though we think we have everything all figured out or that we are "on the right track," the fact of the matter of the matter is, we don't. We aren't.

Life is mystery. Mostly, we don't solve it. All the big questions will assuredly go unanswered: Why do we die? How do we live? What is the universe? How does it work?

The small questions are equally confusing: How will I spend my time today? What will I eat? How will I live? Who will I surround myself with?

Life is but a dream, and we are mostly asleep. If we manage to awaken into consciousness for just a few moments each day, through prayer, or meditation, or trance, or simply by noticing, we find ourselves at the end of this time of connection to the Divine, becoming stunned at the grace and beauty and grief and bliss that each moment holds. In these moments of awakening, our hearts expand outside our bodies. These small slices of consciousness, of seeing "what is," are enough to keep us going.

The tiniest, smallest glimpse of the Divine is enough to fill our hearts; it is enough to allow us to remember what we are.

Also God. Also Divine. Collective soul. All One.

When we understand that we are both human and soul, we also understand that we are dimensional beings—that is, we exist as energy, in all levels and layers and aspects of time, space, matter and concepts that we don't even have a name for yet. Yet even as soul, the mystery of who we are and how we should live does not become any more clear.

What becomes clear is that we don't know.

Yet even in not knowing, we step forward into each day: into the car ride, into the job, into the relationships, into the way we move from one moment to the next, into our lives on this earth.

It is an amazing thing to be both human and soul. The duality, all at once.

If you are not happy in your life, relax your view for a while. If you are happy, don't imagine it will last forever. As a human, you are an electron—buzzing, busy, chaos. Where you will feel best, as human with a human heart, is in the moments of connection: those times of deep stillness when your electron self has gone so fast it has ceased moving, or those times of deep connection, where your self moves so slowly that it can actually listen to the universe.

It does not take much. When you begin to have the smallest glimpse of "what is," you move into consciousness, you move into awakening. The busy, buzzing electron self drops away. And what is left is this: mysterious, mystic, unsolvable you as God, right here on this earth, experiencing everything.

———

If you don't think you feel happy today, relax. Relax into simply being without expectation of holding a certain mood or emotion. That may be enough for this moment. If you are happy, enjoy it. Accept the mystery. Allow your heart to feel everything and open in great thanks.

65
Prayer to the sun

On Kaua'i, we take our bikes out early, maybe as early as 5 am; I don't know. The roosters have awoken us; they are everywhere, chorus of cacophony, noisy and wild.

They wake us up, and we collect our bikes and collect ourselves and head out onto the long winding path above the sea.

It is unimaginable to be in Kaua'i, up at 5 am, already riding a bike.

I have awoken so quickly, and I am so utterly and suddenly awake, that my stomach almost reels from it.

We ride out toward the high cliffs, the better to watch the waves, the better to see the whales that spout and cluster at this time of year.

There are dozens of them, perhaps many more, migrating past the islands, and even the fact that we are there so early, in the half light still, does not preclude us from catching a glimpse—even now, there is the exhale, bursting like sudden foam on the water. Even now, we can spot that.

And the light … it is also lifting.

We continue to ride and soon we are not the only ones. Already the surfers are up, arriving in their cars, before work. We ride past; they are greeting each other, they are carrying their boards, they are standing before the water for a perfect gorgeous second before plunging in to paddle out to the waves and the sea in one giant, joyous breath.

And then, as we round the curve, surfers bobbing like ants on the sea, everything changes.

The sun is rising, the sun is rising, *the sun is rising*!

It is rising in the east like a prayer.

Here on the path, we are paralyzed with the view … the early orb rising right before our eyes. On the beach, the race to the waves continues, the view for the most forgotten—for it is only the sun rising; this is something that happens every day.

A single man stands in reverie. He is in his fifties, sixties, or seventies; it's hard to tell from here. He's not a surfer. He's not here to swim. He's just here to greet the sun; an ordinary man on an ordinary day, wearing an ordinary T-shirt and shorts.

He stands motionless on the beach as we stand motionless above on the cliff, and then the sun is moving up from the horizon, and we see that it is not one man on the beach, but there are suddenly many of us; witnesses to this unutterable moment when the sun rises from dark rim of sea, light pours from infinite horizon, and radiance beams into the world.

I am so awake, I am no longer aware of myself. My heart, my heart! It is captured within the very soul of the sun.

This miracle happens every day. Wherever you are, in every part of the world: light emerges from dark. We receive the blessings of the Universe as the sun births from night.

———

Get up before sunrise. Face the east. Witness the miracle, and claim it as your own with thanks and awe in your heart.

66

The raga of plants

A study was done in which plants were played different kinds of music.[5] Some of the plants were played rock music. Some were played country western. Others were played classical.

The study, done by a music student forced to take required science courses, was scoffed at first; the organization in charge was somewhat embarrassed that the study had even been authorized. However, as these things often happen, the plants themselves began to show such amazing results that the study could no longer be ignored.

The plants did not like rock music, and moved their tendrils away from the source. When they heard a series of notes repeated in sequence without variation 24/7, the plants died. The plants didn't care

---

5. *The Secret Life of Plants*, Peter Tompkins and Christopher Bird, Harper Collins 1973.

one way or another about country music. They moved toward the speakers when classic music was played.

The most interesting thing in my mind, however, was that the plants loved Indian *raga*. More specifically, they loved Indian raga as played by spiritual teacher and musician Ravi Shankar. They moved toward this music. They thrived in this music. They grew bigger, stronger, thicker.

Now, if you have not heard raga, it is a kind of traditional, ancient devotional singing that has a tonal system that can bring out spiritual awakening, spiritual opening, and the highest forms of bliss. It's been sung in temples, in kirtan, for thousands of years. The Beatles brought it to the West in the 1960s after they traveled India and met their guru. It is wildly popular with conscious community all over the world, where people sing it in a modern way. It is available widely on iTunes; in fact, as I write this I am listening to Ravi Shankar's recording "Raga Mishra Gara," and smiling.

It's hard music for the Western ear to hear, but once you get used to it, there's a craving to hear more. As if the soul is so deeply satisfied by this music, so deeply enveloped and expressed, that we are balance or aligned in this music. We become whole.

The tonal scale in this music creates bliss in the human body as it has been doing for thousands of years. This tonal scale also creates bliss in plants, and we would begin to wonder if this is not true of all living beings.

You do not need to learn raga to be in bliss. But it is interesting how music—music of a certain high vibration, music that is spiritual and devotional in its intent—continually creates healing in our bodies, in our minds, in our emotional state and in our very being.

When we listen to this kind of music, something about us becomes whole.

Singing bowls, toning, shamanic percussion, gongs, the crystalline vibrations all possess this high vibration. New Age music that plays the sounds of whales singing or the sounds of space also does. Computers that play mathematical sequences of DNA make the most beautiful music. The sounds of Buddhist monks chanting, the sounds of Indian raga, the newer sounds of healing music—we don't know how it all works. But we are beginning to hear that it does.

———

Listen to some raga today. If you are not sure what to listen to, try Radhe's Dream *by my band* Martyrs of Sound, *or* Queen of Hearts *by Jai Uttal. Put on headphones, relax on your bed, sofa or floor, and spend an entire hour in the healing tones and sensations of this music. You will find your mood lifted, your heart opened, and your sense of gratitude bursting forth for the extraordinary beauty of this life. You may cry at first and then laugh, and then exist simply in peace. This is a way to thrive.*

67

Medium awakened

The mood at Pranafest was tender and sweet: grassy fall meadows, mineral springs burbling through, trees leafy and green.

I'd come to this kirtan and yoga festival in Ashland, Oregon, to be an intuitive reader for the weekend, and I found my assigned spot underneath a beautiful maple—how fortuitous, I thought, setting up my table and chairs, to be sheltered from the sun, to do my work under this dizzying canopy of green.

I did not know yet how lucky I was.

A man arrived and we spoke of his future Beloved.

A woman arrived and we spoke of angels in the southwest.

A man arrived, in need of comfort and hope.

And so on, with people wandering up for readings while the day extended into an experience of absolute flow and bliss. Under the tree, I found myself becoming infused with chlorophyll and oxygen and light, the very heart of the tree pulsing to me by virtue of resting at its roots, relaxing beneath its branches.

Around 3:00 pm, a couple arrived. They were older, not festival goers in the proper sense—they said they'd been passing through at the end of a summer road trip from the east coast, and had stumbled across the festival when they pulled over for a rest stop.

We spoke about intuition, vibration, entities and near death experiences. The woman nodded; the man grimaced uneasily.

"I'm a cynic," he said, ducking his head in embarrassment.

"I used to be a cynic," I agreed. "Until I realized it was all true."

They wandered off and I didn't expect to hear from them again. Sometimes we meet people for a moment, and that's the whole story.

But less than ten minutes later, I looked up to find the man running toward me in an agitated state—not strolling, not walking, but running full force. His face was flushed, tears streaming down, and he threw himself into my vacant chair and began to sob violently with great shuddering and movement, rocking his face in his hands.

"I see dead people," he cried out. "They have messages for me, and they won't leave me alone until I deliver them."

"I'm so afraid," he sobbed. "I have to approach people to give them these messages, and it's so hard … it's so hard! I feel like I'm going crazy."

It was then that I noticed the angels.

They'd appeared suddenly, one to his left, one to his right, the biggest, tallest angels I'd ever seen around a person. Twelve feet tall, twenty feet tall, astonishing figures of blazing white, yet robed, with robes or cording around their chests, and their wings not fully unfurled. They stood behind him looking at me, I realized something big was about to happen.

I reached out, took his hands from his face, clasped his hands in mine, and asked him to be still. I asked him to breathe, and he held my hands as if I would save him. We sat there for many minutes under that sweet, healing tree as the fall air blew around, the sun played softly in the grass, and the angels hovered over this man and opened up his back— they moved close in to work on his heart. We waited in this space under the trees, as the angels tinkered and adjusted and fixed him.

"You're having a healing," I said. "The angels are here," and he nodded and convulsed and the tears were again wet on his cheeks.

They sent me messages to deliver to him too: very clear, arriving into my mind without interference of any kind.

"There will be no more discomfort for you in this work." "The people who need your messages will begin to come to you." "This is your true work."

I received an image of this man within a year, a medium on the west coast, fully immersed in his healing practice.

Finally, I became aware of my own guides: not the usual one or two or four who usually lead me, but a gathering of thirty or forty stacked up behind me in rapt audience, watching in silence as this shifting and healing took place.

The tree held us. It had called this man from the highway, onto the rest area, and into the festival. It attracted him, with all his pain and doubt, to stumble into this time and place where angels were awaiting, ready to do his healing.

We sat there for along time, until the healing was complete, and then we talked quietly about what had happened. When I let go of his hands, a woman walked over to the corner of the table, and spoke to the man.

"Can you tell me about my son?" she asked. "He died two months ago."

And this man who had just been healed by angels, this medium awakened, began to speak to her, and began his work.

———

Many times in your life, you have taken a detour for reasons you did not understand, and miracles have happened when you arrived. Think back to these times. Recall again what happened. Give thanks to these unexpected moments that brought you to exactly where you needed to be.

68
Kundalini rising

I went out of body again at Jai Uttal, many years after my first Krishna Das concert. It was nearly a decade later in fact, during which time I'd experienced many out of body experiences, many explosions of Kundalini, many trances and experiences in which my consciousness went to a soul level.

But none as big as this.

I would like to say I was an entirely different person after so many years of practice, but I was not. Better, perhaps, but still packed with flaws and foibles and failings. Better, perhaps, but still prone to fear and anxiety and worry and anger and...you get the picture.

I've seen Jai Uttal many times; he's my favorite kirtan leader. I've seen him in small venues, I've seen him at big concerts, I've spent a week in workshop with him at the Esalen Institute high on the cliffs of Big Sur where the waves pound and the sun shines and you can't believe you're not in a heaven of some sort, the way the rest of the world simply falls away when you're there.

But in this case, Jai Uttal drove in the festival gates under cover of dusk sliding into darkness, on the night when the full moon blazed over an outdoor stage and he hung out in the makeshift green room tent while the other performers went through their paces. He was wearing the same silver-gray ski jacket he'd worn last time, and his hair had gone white, or grayish white, in the past year.

It was cold in the audience; I'd been sitting on a thin blanket on top of barren ground so damp it was nearly muddy. When Jai finally started I was chilled already, my arms cold, my back starting to ache. But then the kirtan began, and I stood up with everyone else and began to dance, and something about it all moved me: the fir trees above, the great clean coldness of the night, the full moon rising such that you see it hanging in one position, and then another place later on in the deep night sky, rising, rising, rising, this ball of mystery and wonder and amazement as the music poured into my body and into my soul.

I'd had a busy day at the festival, doing readings for people. I had not eaten lunch or dinner yet. It was late at night, later than I am usually up. I was cold. And even so, as I danced, I felt a burning begin from the inside, a change in the way energy was moving in my body. Jai had been singing for nearly an hour, I'd been dancing and chanting that whole time, the full moon had risen high over the stage, and suddenly I felt something burst open: it was my heart.

And following that, another feeling, as my breath suddenly shifted to an involuntary deepening, a kind of power huffing and blowing, so that I was inadvertently breathing in and out at the deepest level and something began to rise from stomach, from my back, from my bowels, up through my heart and throat and mind and all my consciousness broke free of my body at once, so that my body stopped its crazy, frantic, wild dancing and my voiced stopped its crazy, frantic, wild singing, and there was suddenly a kind of *whoosh* from in to out, from down to up, and everything came out: all the heart, all the energy, all the intellect, all the prayer, all of it, and I found myself suspended, motionless, with all the stars of the Universe, all the energy of the cosmos, all the particulate of everything, myself exploded into pure consciousness outside my body. I hung in that state for a long time. I do not know if I moved or stopped or saw.

I was simply there, as soul.

I did not feel separate from myself, as I had that first time at Krishna Das when I went out of body. This time, body came with— I expanded and became one with Universe/Divine/One/All.

I felt like God feels every day. And I understood I could feel like this every day, if I just keep practicing, opening, being. I wept in gratitude, for this experience and this understanding, and the full moon shone down upon me.

My partner showed up at this moment, pushing through the crowd to get to me. He'd brought a mysterious vegan chocolate dessert on a soggy paper plate. If you've read much of my writing, you have noticed by this time that this man tends to show up right around the time I've headed out of body and am coming back in, with a hand to hold or a dessert to eat!

I chomped down the sweet and it was good, and the moon looked amazing, and up on stage Jai was still singing his heart out. I threw my arms open and laughed and laughed.

What a life this is! What amazement and joy!

———

When was the last time you felt pure, unadulterated joy of simply being? This is yours to experience every day, many times a day. There are so many ways to get there: affection, sex, love, kindness, music, dance, yoga, exercise, nature, writing, praying, meditating ... all ways of reaching bliss and opening in your life. Try one, even if it is not your normal way, and even if you cry a little bit at first. Try one, until the bliss takes over, and you can't help but be grateful for the experience of your life.

69

Spontaneous Buddha

Perhaps you've heard about those people who can't wear watches, who fry toasters, and who cause all kinds of machinery to blow up whenever they're near, just because of the particular way their body energy is wired?

In recent months, I have turned into one of those people.

I've blown up my car battery, set off smoke alarms, caused the washing machine to turn on and the dishwasher to turn off. Don't even ask about the toaster.

We laugh when we watch movies in which the face of Jesus is imprinted on a tortilla and the village goes crazy, or shows up in the mold on a shower wall, and the TV crews head in. We giggle at the improbability of a healing spring suddenly gushing forth from the ground, or a statue weeping tears, or any other sort of impossible miracle happening. And yet, these things do happen.

Angels are among us, in ways and numbers that we cannot imagine. They work in the ethers. They are actively involved in the electronica; the energies that we all use for communication and machinery these days. In fact, there is so much rubbing of elbows with the angelic realm, it's surprising we aren't tripping over each other all day long.

Until we are conscious, there is a veil of perception that makes it impossible for us to see. And yet when we become conscious, that veil is lifted. This happens especially during a near death experience or other shock to the system, when we suddenly realize that there is more to the Universe than we have ever dreamed.

And then, miracles show up out of nowhere, and we simply understand that *this is how it is.*

While I was writing this morning, my phone suddenly began to vibrate on my desk, and when I picked it up, I saw it was playing a movie of Buddha. There was Buddha, serene faced in stone, and there was water pouring over him like a fountain, the sound of the water gurgling from my phone.

I held the phone in my hand, not sure what I was seeing.

This image, this movie of Buddha, did not come from a phone call. It was not a link. It was not embedded, or in my photo gallery, or bookmarked, or a message. It was not a YouTube video, or from any other recognizable source.

It was not an image I had ever seen before, and it was not stored in or sent to my phone.

It just showed up, Buddha, in healing water, sent as a message to me.

Sometimes, these things happen. We call them miracles now, because we don't understand, we still don't fathom, that we exist in the magic all the time.

Spontaneous Buddha. Spontaneous Jesus. Spontaneous spirit, guide, ascended master, saint, holy one. Spontaneous starting of the washing machine. Spontaneous movie on the smart phone.

Miracles are with us at all times, if we are open to see.

———

Today, watch for spontaneous miracles. Instead of searching for reasons why it is not possible, or how it was circumstantial, simply allow yourself to be in wonder.

Life is mystery. Miracles are everywhere.

70
Dreamtime

In our dreams, we are able to see things our daily mind does not allow.

It is in the relaxation of sleep that we are able to easily drift to the layers and levels of consciousness in which our dreams are revealed.

It is in the relaxation of sleep that we allow our hearts this vulnerability: to see what our minds don't allow.

In ancient times, we retreated to the cave or hut to be safe through the night from predators prowling outside in the night.

We created fire, to light the dark through the night. We hunkered down in our dwelling, and pulled coverings around us, and clung close to the other beings we slept with.

At dawn, when we arose with the sun, our dreams still hung on us like cobwebs. We sat gently before the fire, waking from dreamtime into today time, and as we shifted from one consciousness to the other, our dreams penetrated into us with meaning.

Nowadays, we are inside most of the time. We create light with a flip of the switch. Our predators are things like worry, anxiety and confusion.

We don't always rise early to sit with our dreams; or if we do get up early, we're up with the buzz of a smart phone, running with a cup of coffee in hand to our "to do" list and schedule. In this way, our dreams are wrenched from us as we leap from bed. We do not allow the mystery of the gentle time to permeate back to our souls.

In dreams our understanding is illuminated. We receive symbols, images, emotions, meaning, understanding, messages, Divine downloads, healings.

We see the people we know, or people we once knew. We are often visited by angels, spirit guides, and holy ones. We often see the departed.

In dreamtime, we are able to understand things with a clarity that is not available to us in everyday reality; at least, it is not available to most of us, when we are hurried, rushed, pressured, and anxious in our daily lives.

If you are actively dreaming, take these dreams as a gift. Get up slowly and quietly in the morning, with time to sit with your dreams. Unpack your dreams each morning with writing or meditation as you might open a package that contains a small jewel of light. Not everything will be clear. But these nightly messages, when allowed to permeate daily awareness, will help to transform you.

If you think you're not dreaming, or can't remember your dreams, ask yourself why. What is it that you're afraid to have revealed to you, in your vulnerable, open state of slumber? What is it that you are resistant to receive from your very soul?

Begin to change habits that prevent dreaming: substances, electronica, worry, anxiety, looping thoughts, lack of joyous experiences, being too busy. To sleep soundly and to dream actively is one of the easiest ways for the Divine to bring you the teachings and healings that you most require.

Don't worry overmuch about interpreting your dreams with a book filled with categories and definitions. Instead, unpack your dreams in your own heart. You know what they mean to you. Or if you don't know yet, you are being informed.

———

Tonight before you go to sleep, hold the intention that you will remember your dreams in the morning. When you awaken, wake slowly and gratefully, and allow your dreams to stay with you as long as you can. Be quiet and still, staying in the dawning state as long as you can. The longer you can do this, the more clearly your dreams will come to you, and the more easily you will receive their messaging.

71
The container of our lives

What makes our lives important is that they are finite.

We are born into the world; it's the only entrance possible. Someday we'll die; it's our only way out. In between, we are each given a container of days, years, or decades that is the sum of our lives.

Some of us will get an "easy" life; others will face challenge after challenge. To a certain point, we create our own experience by the choices we make—what we choose to do or not do. But much of what happens is Divine destiny—a trajectory through time that we neither can predict nor fully understand.

Such is the mystery.

As we move from birth to death, our challenge is to make something meaningful of our lives. On the surface, most of us do: we make progress in a career, get married, create a family, travel the world or complete any of the other milestones we might consider "adult."

And it's not all that hard, either. For what seems like an insurmountable challenge at age twenty or thirty, often becomes reality by mid-life. The achieving of "success" just took time: getting up in the morning to the six o'clock alarm, slamming back coffee and blasting off to the office, the worksite, or to take care of the kids at home. Lather, rinse, repeat.

Day after day we do the dance. Our to-do list gets bigger and more complicated. Over time, success comes. We have a job, a place to live, a family—whatever the particular emblems of adulthood we choose to wear. Or if we don't choose to have any of these, we create a life busy with experiences: trips to far-off places, adventures.

It's good to work. It's good to have a family. It's good to do adventures. Yet at a certain point we realize that in order to experience life at a deeper level, we must focus on something quite a bit bigger.

The great saints and holy ones teach us to look at the trajectory of our lives as a process of soul growth: the Divine self in human body, facing all that humans face, turning continually away from petty mundane perspective to spiritual perspective.

We spend a lot of time thinking about what we're going to do next, what we're going to create next, who we want to be with next, where we want to travel next, and when we put our minds to it, we accomplish these things, to a degree. But the true meaning of our lives is not about houses or family or trips to Nepal. By the time we reach a certain age, whether it's 34, 48, or 93, we'll have a slew of accomplishments and experiences under our belt. But when we look back, we'll be shocked at how quickly time has passed.

All those six o'clock alarms. And in the blink of the eye, our live's been lived.

Many times, we may have been past thinking or future thinking so very much, so busy out there amassing things and people and adventures, that we've forgotten to enjoy what's right in front of us in each moment.

We're each given a container—the container we receive is a part of our soul agreement, our Divine destiny. In this time between birth and death, we have a chance to live as fully ourselves as we can dare to be. In this container, we have the chance to be awake to both gravitas and the joy of our lives, and to become grateful beyond understanding.

———

What are the most meaningful ways you have filled the container of your life? What are the least important? If you had ten years left to live, what would you do differently? Five years? Twenty? Consider your container today and how you would like to fill it.

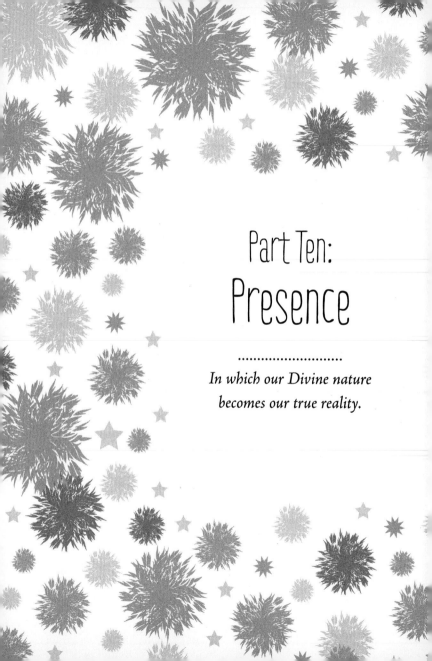

Part Ten:
Presence

....

*In which our Divine nature
becomes our true reality.*

72
Lending a hand

There was once a man who had been sentenced to forty years in prison, for a victimless crime. He'd been incarcerated when he was forty-seven, for something not particularly heinous, an accounting sleight of hand, something that hadn't hurt anyone in particular, just changed the ways the numbers added up. At seventy-nine, he was bent and exhausted, with just a handful of years left to go. There was a picture of him in his cell: a slight, weakened fellow in grainy black and white, leaning back on his plain bed, hands behind his head. A week before, they'd told him his sentence was up; it was time for him to leave. Because of his inordinately good behavior and his advancing years, they'd told him, his sentence had been scrapped. He'd done his time. He was free to go.

"But I like it here," he told them. There was food to eat, he was well treated. This has become my home, he said. I'm used to things here.

They escorted him out and gave him his belongings, an old steel money clip and a sports coat that did not fit, and they drove him to the front gate. He walked away like a refugee, a displaced person with no destination in mind. At one time there had been plans to live with a sister, but she had died a year earlier, and the house had been sold. There was no next of kin.

He stood, hunched in the wind, and cried by the side of the road. "You're my family," he said. "I'm too old to move."

When the warden went home that night, ensconced in his Ford Explorer, he noticed that the prisoner was still there, huddled motionless by the road. The next morning, when the warden drove back in, the man was gone. Nobody ever knew more than that.

———

There are times you've been displaced in your own life. There are times you've seen others who have been displaced. Did someone lend you a hand, or were you ignored? Have you lent a hand to others, or ignored them? When we understand we are all One, and that what affects one affects us all, we look at each other with new eyes.

73
The unending cycle

There was an afternoon some years ago when my partner and I walked into the trees. There were older trees in the forest we traveled, some yews a thousand years old. There were elder oaks, old madronas, maples, evergreens, and pines. We walked into a gathering of trees who had existed there for decades, if not centuries, and I was stunned by their knobby arms waving, just beginning to leaf out into spring.

In this circle of brown and green, I saw that ferns were beginning to overtake the bark, symbols of decay giving way to new life. Lichens draped down from every twiggy limb, more proof of nature's symbiotic, endless way—every stage beautiful, every stage a mix of life with death, death with life.

We do not always remember the cycle of nature when we are so busy in our human form, so busy living and shaving away the signs of lichen, lifting the ferns from our body with chemicals and cosmetics and treatments. We fit into incrementally larger or smaller clothing over time, and even if our clothing is the same size, it fits differently: no longer sleekly upon our musculature, but straining or slacking over humps and knobs as we wizen and fall, gravity pulling our skin, our backs and shoulders hunching into the ways we have always stood, like trees who turn their limbs only to the sun, only to find that they have grown only on one side.

So we stand, our own arms outstretched.

As I stood in this circle of trees, I could hear them whispering or talking or singing. I do not know which. I could hear the murmur of them clearly, clearly understood to me as a passionate wave of understanding. *We are here. We are here*, they seemed to say.

My face was wet with listening, tears streaming without knowledge of tears. *We are here.* I am listening.

————

Head to a park, the woods, even your own back yard. Observe a tree closely: at the bark, at the branches, and notice where there are signs of new life growing on old. See where there are signs of decay and death, in which new life bursts forward, Consider how your own body is changing, and how life is always changing, and how life as consciousness does not end, ever. Death begets life. Give thanks for your understanding of this eternal cycle of nature.

74
Rest stop

There are thousands of rest areas built into the U.S. road system. Most people simply think of them as a convenient place to get a cheap cup of coffee, to use the cement restrooms with their warped, non-breakable mirrors, or to walk the dog in the area marked "PETS." Most don't realize that people live here.

For three years, I made a weekly eighty-mile trip north up I-5 to do sessions for folks in Portland. I always stopped at the rest area—and it was then that I began to notice them: the regulars.

The gray-haired woman with the denim shirt who sometimes sat inside her car, and sometimes stood near the women's restroom.

The tall, skinny man with scraggly black hair who hovered near the trash can at the south side of the men's bathroom, talking and gesticulating at the trees in the distance.

The older, grizzled man with the denim jacket who sat between the men's and women's restroom, often on the cement but sometimes on a chair, with his black guitar case open for donations. He played guitar and sang a litany of indistinguishable country songs that had no beginning, no end, as if by sheer tenacity he might be able to sing his way to a donation. He didn't look up, he didn't look out, he focused on his fingers making each of the chords: A, E, G; E, G, A and so on, and so on.

It wasn't fancy, it wasn't enjoyable, it was work for him, and it was work for the drivers who walked by in a hurry to do their bathroom break and get back on the road. Even in the short time I watched him, I could see men shaking their heads as they passed him, and the women looking everywhere else.

I don't remember when I first noticed this man; if it was the first year or the second. But at some point, I began to see him every time I was there and it dawned on me that he lived there.

He lived in the small rust-colored hatchback with the tape over the back window, always parked in the spaces closest to the restrooms. The inside was stuffed with every kind of blanket and box. Also inside was the woman in the denim shirt—his wife or girlfriend or traveling companion.

They lived in the car, he played guitar by the restrooms and I came to notice later that sometimes she also begged, standing in her spot by the woman's restroom with a cardboard sign in her hand.

The couple was there like clockwork. They were there in the summer when it was too hot. They were there in the winter when it was too cold to be without a coat. They were there in the spring and fall when it did nothing but rain.

I'm certain there were patrols, authorities that would require that these two to move along. But perhaps they had it timed so well: this rest stop for this much time, another one down the road at a different time, working their way up and down I-5 with such systematic planning that they were not considered an issue or a problem. Or perhaps there were so many homeless in those years, the authorities looked the other way.

During the end of the third year, I'd gotten too busy to make the weekly trip to Portland as my work expanded. I drove up one last Wednesday, and made my usual stop.

Sure enough, the man was there playing guitar, but the woman wasn't around. I sat in my car as I often did, watching for her. The hatchback was there, but she wasn't in it. She wasn't standing by the woman's restroom.

In fact, I didn't see her at all.

Suddenly, I saw the man get up, put his guitar down and head over to the place where the scraggly man usually stood. He rubbed his eyes as if there was something in them, and he put his hands on his hips and arched his stiff body back, as if trying to get some relief. After a moment, he sat back down, but the same thing happened; his hand flew to his eyes. A man stopped and asked if he was okay. A woman came over, and then she took a wad of cash out of her wallet and put it in his hand. He took the money, and seemed to brighten. But after the woman had gone, he stood up again, agitated with his hands to his face, and I realized he was crying.

And then I realized, the woman was gone. Maybe she'd left, or maybe she'd died—gotten sick in the rain and cold. She'd died here at this rest stop, or at one down the road. And this homeless man was carrying on the only way he could.

He picked up the guitar and started singing again, his voice strained with hoarseness. People walked by, sometimes tossing money into his guitar case, sometimes not. Every now and then, he broke down again. Drivers got out of their cars and back into their cars, a steady stream who only saw him for an instant: that man playing guitar by the restroom.

But he was so much more.

———

You will pass many people today who have stories that are as deep, compli-cated, intense, sad, rich and joyous as your own. Everyone has experienced the same depth of feeling as you have—you are not the only one. Look intently at the human being who is in front of you today and recognize this. Recognize it again and again, and give thanks we are all here together.

75
Miracle glasses

In late 2012, I am diagnosed with a melanoma.

There has been a new, strange mole on my shoulder since the fourth of July, and now it is early October.

The mole—slightly odd, a little worrisome—was removed yesterday, and the lab results are back already. The nurse on the phone doesn't say, "It will be okay." Instead she says, "I'm sorry."

I sit with the news, trying to figure out what, how, why. None of these questions come back with any answers.

On the sixth of July, my mother went into the ICU where she remained for six weeks. On the 25th of July, my daughter had scoliosis surgery from which she is still recovering. During this time of medical crisis in our family, the mole grew.

And even as I sit with the news, I astonished by my physical reaction: my stomach rebels, my hands become clammy, my head spins, and fear implodes within me. At the same time, I realize I am having nearly the same reaction I had during my first near death experience in 2000.

There's this sense of blessing, blessing, blessing over everything. What a life this is! What a life I have been given!

I'm ready to go if it's my time. If this is my calling, I feel complete—drenched and infused with the blessings I have had. But oh! I want to stay! Not for myself. But for my family, my partner, my work.

When I look at my life with my miracle glasses on, it's all been one big miracle after another. Even when I forget to put those rosy tints on, it's still been so many days and months and years and decades of awesome.

Not every single moment has been great; I've suffered my share of anger, fear, and pain, just like anyone else.

But the things I have experienced, the situations I have encountered, the people I have met, the relationships I have been in, the emotions I have felt; all I have seen and known and existed in; the good, the bad, the all of it—this is human life lived big.

Now, compared to some, you might say that I've lived small:

I haven't yet traveled much. I haven't yet been rich. I'm average in looks and figure. I've mostly been a mother. My work—my true work—has only arrived to me in the past decade, a flurry of writing and teaching. I've never bungee jumped or traveled to India or visited Machu Picchu or any of those things a person might have on a bucket list. But even in this small container, this smaller, quieter container of my life, the miracles that have come to pass are rich and full and astounding.

When I think about the doctor appointment ahead in which more will be determined, I veer again into panic. Again, it is not for myself. I have been abundantly blessed, extravagantly gifted. But there is so much I would like to support and love—the relationships in my life, the soul crossings that are my karma. For these people, for my children and partner—I want to be here. For my clients, my work, I want the same.

Life…what an oddity, what a mystery! This consciousness, this heart, this body. I'd like to experience more.

On days like this, where death is brought to our door, we can choose fear, or we can choose to put on our miracle glasses and look at things another way. Even when it gets personal. Even when it's your own mortality, nudging you in the arm.

This gift of existence is beyond comprehension. This chance to live as Divine soul in earth body, and all of the lessons and experiences and emotions and soul growth this entails.

I head out to the trees and open my arms wide and I say it loud, and I say it clearly: thank you, thank you, and more thank you.

———

Put on your miracle glasses. Review every blessing in your life. Not the things. Not even the people. But all of the millions of experiences you have had over time. Say thank you until you are done saying thank you. Then say thank you some more.

76
Heaven's ledger

What if everything you might consider as your life's purpose was nothing? What if all your accomplishments, when you arrived for your reckoning in heaven, nirvana, beyond the veil, wherever you believe you are going…what if these were taken out, examined, and found to be nothing—no longer shiny and bright but drab and shabby, as if collected and carted in an old grocery bag?

What if they were looked at—all your pretty things—and then discarded to float away on the breeze, the bright white tail of one particularly favorite accomplishment sent flapping, pale and gentle as a kite rising? Everything taken out and looked at and discarded, until when you reached the bottom of the bag, there was nothing left.

Nothing.

Nothing counted enough to be considered your finest accomplishment. Nothing counted enough to be considered your finest achievement. Your whole illustrious, successful, important, rewarded life was determined a wash. Nothing counted. You arrived with nothing.

And still they let you in.

There may or may not be a pearly gate to heaven, guarded by St. Peter. There may or may not be a time of reckoning with points tallied up, sins examined under a celestial microscope. It is your choice to believe in this version of the afterlife or not—for really, what does anyone know?

Few have crossed the line and returned to tell. And what they do tell—of white tunnels, bright light and angels—doesn't seem to include a ledger in the clouds for "naughty" and "nice."

When you lift off from the idea of right or wrong, good or bad, take punitive moralistic views out of the equation, and focus instead on heart's opening into compassion, connection, love…this becomes the true measure of our lives.

Not what job we had, but how much we cared for others.

Not how much money we made, but how much we loved.

Not how many trips we took, but how much we enjoyed.

———

If you were to look at your life outside of the usual bucket list of achieve-ments and experiences, how does your life measure? How much has your heart opened thus far? How much more would you like it to open into gratitude for what you have experienced thus far? Start today: simply ask for this opening into thanks.

77
Angels in the road

We are driving the winding mountain road to Crater Lake, Oregon, elevation 8,000 feet. The day is wild with early autumn; trees becoming drier and more scraggly with every rise, giving way to scrub and rocks, then finally mostly rocks.

The signs along the road remind us of what comes after fall: "Snowfall: 45 feet," one reads, and tall poles set as snowplow guides remain here year round to remind us.

How could there be snow here? I wonder, and then I remember: everything changes. In a moment, the sky opens and a single flake falls and suddenly we are blanketed with a new reality. Everything changes in a moment.

We do not know which moment this will be. The road is curving in a way that requires all my concentration, and when two motorcyclists appear behind me, I find a pullout and veer over to let them pass, surprised at how slippery the gravel is; how awkward it feels to be sliding on the gravel. A movie flashes in my mind, and then the thought: *I hope they don't crash.*

In three more curves we see it: the biker lying in the middle of the road, two motorcycles stacked to the side, a car parked on the shoulder. We park precariously, and race toward them.

It could be anything: injury, trauma, death. We can't tell yet.

Three people huddle over the biker, and there is blood: a trail about eight feet long streaming from her body, both dark red and bright in the sun. It looks funny there, incongruous. Everything on this road is clear and hard, and yet this blood flows like a vibrant jewel, like liquid rubies. My mind slips sideways. I remember to breathe.

The biker, a woman in her fifties, has certainly broken her leg. Her left foot hangs precariously. There is a flap of skin under her chin, a gash under her thigh that seeps through her pants, and who knows what else. Her helmet is off, and she is crying *owee, owee, owee,* in the way that a child of about seven might cry. This relieves me; she is conscious, she is here, she is alive.

The situation becomes more focused. The man at her leg and the woman at her head are both ICU nurses. The other man in leather motorcycle jacket is her partner. They are stemming the blood, talking to her, and the ambulance will be here soon. I am ready for anything, and yet I see quickly that I am not needed in this immediate space. I turn my attention down the road and begin to direct traffic.

There are angels here, Divine energies orchestrating this entire experience: the coincidence of two ICU nurses driving to Crater Lake in the same car, beginning their trip at a certain time, driving at a certain pace, stopping or not stopping along the way, so that in the exact moment that the rocks glint and the woman skids on the gravel, the ICU nurses arrive at the accident scene—it's the very next curve in the road, and these earth angels have arrived with training and skills to save lives.

We stay and direct traffic until the emergency teams arrive: the park ranger, the ambulance, the life flight helicopter is on its way. Only then do we leave.

When we reach Crater Lake, the air feels too thin, and maybe it is. We stop at the lodge but the normalcy, the luxury, the everyday, the inability to see life as precarious is too much to breathe. The trail of rubies on the road still crowds my mind.

We walk to the viewpoint and gaze at the lake, letting the blue fill our eyes. It's all lake and sky and horizon, a lake formed one day eight thousand years ago by a giant crater falling to earth. In one moment, something fell from the sky, and in that moment, everything changed.

There is a sense of angels here. There is the sense of entities at an etheric level and power I have never before experienced. These beings are not concerned with my life; they are enormous, extraordinary, powerful, tending to the charges of the earth, the sky, the atmosphere, the energies. The energy moves differently here—higher, faster, brighter, wilder, not human.

We are in the ethers, looking down at this lake of impossible blue. Somewhere, the biker is traveling through the same stunning air on a life flight helicopter, scared and adrenalized and in pain and in bliss that she is still alive, not understanding yet how her life has changed, but knowing that it has changed entirely.

———

Anything can happen, at any time, to any of us. But there is no need to fear: there will be angels who arrive ready to help, at the exact moment they are needed. Can you recall a time in your life when you were helped by angels? Can you remember when you were the angel? Close your eyes, and recall this memory for a moment, and notice how you feel.

78

I see you

When you witness a loved one in an intensive care unit, you see the real person. All armor taken off. All shields down.

In this way, sitting bedside in an ICU, machines whirring, alarms beeping, can be one of the biggest blessings to a relationship you can have.

One summer evening my mother was out having drinks on the deck with her friends. The weather was brilliant: balmy, breezy, the kind of midsummer's night you hold close all year. A few hours later, she was transported in the back of an ambulance to the hospital; the details are too complicated to list here.

By the time I drove up, she was fully installed in the ICU: tubes entering every orifice, someone else's blood transfusing into her veins, kidneys on full dialysis, oxygen dialed way up.

I got the call from my brother, panicked like I'd never seen him before. He held the phone to her mouth so she could talk to me, and she insisted I not come. "I'm fine," she said. "Don't bother making the trip."

I was on the road within two hours, battling it up I-5. It is myth that by moving away to the neighboring town, or cross-country, or even out of country, that we are ever free of our connection to our parents.

This is a karmic connection, born into us in our blood.

ICU.

I see you.

I see you in all your vulnerability. I see you with all your faults. I see you as a human being. I see you teetering at the edge of a cliff, hoping and praying that nobody will push you off. I see you stepping back from death, then teetering again, back and then forth, for two whole days.

It was a long 48 hours.

The body is so precarious: the breath, the heart, the vital signs. Every system on my mother had gone wrong except her mind.

There is a particular way she covers her mouth with her hands; this is a gesture that I also do, and that my own children do. We use it to express uncertainty or confusion. In the ICU, my mother's hands fluttered over her mouth, landing and relanding like birds.

Where am I? What is wrong with me? Am I going to die?

These are the questions my mother fluttered through as the drugs and machines worked their collective work to save her. To witness another person approach the realization of mortality is a transformation in itself.

In the end, my mother got out of the ICU. She graduated to a regular hospital bed, and then to rehab and finally, after six weeks of medical care, she was able to move home with help.

During her illness, she changed. She became softer, sweeter, more patient. Less sharp, less strong, more kind. In the passage through the darkest house, she discovered light. She did not fully transform, she did not become ablaze with light as happens to some. But she had allowed the light in, a small lantern of realization. For her to mull on in her own way.

Sometimes, being in an ICU lets us see the other person fully, in all their vulnerability and need. Sometimes, the ICU lets a person see themselves in a new way.

Whenever we become vulnerable to each other, whether the cause is emergency or conscious intention, the result is light and love.

———

Have you been witness to someone with serious illness? To someone nearing death? The changes that happen from these experiences are not always about the body. The most important changes happen in the soul. Consider today how you allow vulnerability from others, how you are also vulnerable, and how your heart opens in thanks whenever you do either.

79
Prayer Flags

There's a basket full on the top shelf of an ancient Chinese cabinet—it's burnished black with myriad tiny drawers which even now contain the residue of herbs and Oriental medicines. I'm in an import store in Oregon, and the entire floor is filled with antiques from other times, other places.

The prayer flags in the basket are an afterthought, meant to be an impulse buy, something fun and affordable. They're bright and shiny and packed so neatly, in a crinkly plastic that's hard to find in America; cellophane, we might call it. It's not flimsy or slippery, but it is meant to endure, to travel safely in the cargos of ocean-crossing ships or freight airplanes.

I pick up a package for my older daughter. They're Tibetan prayer flags, the label says, from Nepal. Handmade by people many thousands of miles away, a symbol of hope that flies from gompas, stupas, the rooftop of temples; they are strewn from gates and at high mountain crossings. In the U.S., they are tacked to the insides of retail stores, displayed on the porches of bungalows, tied to the balcony railings of student apartments.

These tiny colored flags are meant to fray and tatter in the wind. The elements greet them, and add to their story. In this particular pack, there's a flag in every color of the chakras, with simple mantras written carefully in block letters on each flag. The messages, the prayers, the wishes are clear:

Success. Peace. Knowledge. Prosperity. Long life.

They're strewn on twine so thin, I wonder how it will withstand the winds. But I know this is the nature of prayer flags: to be strung without regard for protection or care. They're all prayers, sent on the wind, released in the very breath of wishing.

I also know these prayer flags have a purpose far greater than the breath of wishes.

They are meant to remind us: I was here. I suffered this. I experienced this. I knew this. I existed. I was. These were my hopes, my dreams, my wishes, my cares. These, these, these. We string the prayer flags all over the world, not because we are Buddhist, or because we are from Nepal, but because these tiny bits of fabric and string are set to flutter in places so that we may see, bear witness, remember.

Hope, connection, love … Our deepest wishes borne onto the wind. Not just your own. But everyone's. To see these flags fluttering somewhere, anywhere, is to know that all prayers, all wishes are shouted out for all the Universe to hear.

We are infinitely connected in the knowing of each other's hearts.

———

Watch for prayers today. Not just yours, but the prayers of others. The deeply held wishes. The deepest hopes and dreams. Watch for these in wonderment, and be reminded again with deepest gratitude of how our heart is all the same.

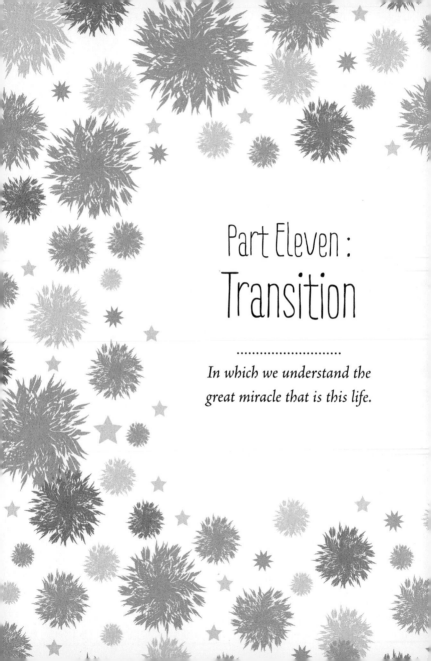

Part Eleven:
Transition

....

In which we understand the
great miracle that is this life.

80
An ordinary day

Most of us don't know the day we'll die. We just know we will.

I met Riva years ago when I was doing a lot of dancing. By dancing, I don't mean the formal kind with steps and choreography and timing. Instead, I mean ecstatic dance: free movement to find awareness, opening, bliss.

I'd go to dance workshops at retreat centers in nature: the woods, the mountains, the ocean. I would stay the weekend, becoming for a few days part of newly met dancers, kindred spirits who also liked to move as their meditation. Often we'd share rooms to save money. A bunk room, a sleeping bag room we'd share with someone we didn't know.

I met Riva that way; a shared room box checked on the registration form. When I arrived to our little cabin in the woods, she'd taken the bed to the left and I was reserved the bed to the right. It was a plain, spare room, as these rooms often are; "rustic" might be the word on the brochure. But even though it was already alarmingly chilly outside, the room was warmed up for me; Riva had dialed up the heat in welcome.

She wasn't there when I arrived, but her presence was loud and clear. The bed was neatly made up with linens she'd brought from home: a cozy hand-sewn quilt, and a lumpy pillow probably taken straight from her own bed.

Her suitcase was unpacked; everything was neatly hung from the pegs in the wall. And there on the small wooden shelf under the window, she'd set out her treasure: pictures of her children and husband.

She'd even brought work with her, which surprised me. We'd all be so busy dancing, doing the workshop, I couldn't imagine getting anything else done.

But there were her books on naturopathy ... big, thick, complicated text books, with pages marked and tabbed to study.

"It's my life dream," she told me later that night, after a long day of dancing as I settled down for a long sleep. She hefted up a book and turned her reading light so it wouldn't bother me. "I've always wanted to be a naturopath, and someday I will."

And someday, she was.

Riva treated many people in the years to follow. She danced, and she raised her kids, and she loved her husband, and she healed soul after soul in her work. I didn't see her for many years. Her life was full, busy.

And then one day, I got the news that Riva had died. She'd had a heart attack out of the blue. It was an ordinary day, she'd been working. She transitioned before the EMTs arrived.

Sometimes we meet these bright, bright spirits who are lit from within. They move quickly through life, and they're given all the joys they can handle. And then they're gone, just as fast.

Riva is missed by people every day; not just her family, but so many that she touched. I sometimes think back to that night, when we talked quietly and easily from our separate beds in the little cabin with the trees waving and swaying above.

If I'd known Riva was going to die a few years later, would I have acted differently? I don't know. But I do know it was a gift to have a moment with Riva, with her quilt and her pictures and her books all around her, on an ordinary day.

————

You will meet people who are going to die soon. You will meet people who will seem to live forever. You don't know how much time you have with anyone. Each moment is a gift. Open these gifts in gratitude.

81

Beyond the veil

Death does not change much. It is as simple as sliding behind the veil.

The veil is pale yellow or golden, shimmering with light. Some say it looks like a shower curtain, and I am afraid to report that they are right.

You can pull the veil open or closed at will. The people who pass through, who come to this place beyond the veil...they may or may not stay there for long.

It is like a holding pen, a gathering place, a train station, or a giant entrance hall, where you wait, with others, until it is your time to move to the next place.

You don't have to be dead to see it. You can access this other dimension, this separate universe, at any time. At least many of you can.

Those who are more advanced or who have learned the trick can casually close their eyes and in a simple, effortless movement flick the filmy, shimmering shower curtain open, a gentle clacking and rolling as it moves...well, these same people can also slide back and forth between the worlds: earth world, spirit world, present, future, past, life, death, and what is indubitably beyond death, beyond imagining, all matter, all energy in perfect blissful union.

But even for the others who do not yet have the knack...sometimes, this can happen too. For the veil is always fluttering. And sometimes, there is a small gap, like what you see when you look at the parting of clouds on a bright summer day, and you imagine that you can see God. Sometimes, this happens. When you least expect it, without effort or knowledge a crack appears, as if someone has left the curtain open for just a second, and you can see into the next dimension.

It is at this moment that glimpses of other worlds, our ancestors, the people we love who have passed on, the future, the infinite, the eternal now, become possible. Even for those who are not paying attention. Even those who refuse to look.

Sometimes, you can see them just behind the veil—everyone you ever loved who has died, waiting there in the great gathering hall, milling around and talking to each other, and they might greet you too, their faces will light up as you see them, and they can see you.

You can pull the curtain open—try it now.

Breathe in. Breathe out. Look at the hum of particles hanging in the air. We are all this, this hum and drone. The smallest things shift and move, they fizz and gather. It is the same everywhere. It is all like this. Look with new eyes.

Close your eyes, and imagine that you can see a golden veil to the next realm. Now, using your mind, pull that veil open. Sense, feel and see what is there. Do you see a loved one who has departed? The veil is movable; death is not an end. Try this technique in the next days with thanks in your heart that you can see in this way now, or will be able to in time.

82

Homecoming

When people get ready to transition into spiritual form, you may begin to notice changes in the way they experience the other dimensions.

This seeing beyond the veil may mean death is near, or it may be simply foresight of a more distant future to come; we are not always privy to the details of Divine timing.

In 2012, during the summer that my mother nearly died, she experienced such a transformation. The veil lifted away for her.

The first change was in her personality. Even as her body was wracked with medical problems, she became more clear. She lost the fear that had plagued her so long, and became almost childlike in her sweetness. It was as if I saw her as true spirit flame for the first time; I began to see her as a little girl of about age seven or eight, without all her cares and worries—a child full of hope.

I visited her often that summer at the nursing home and did my best to provide decoration for the drab brown walls, the beige curtains, the old furniture. It was clean, the staff was warm, but the décor was depressing. I opened the blind on her window and pushed it open for fresh air. She had a view out to the street, where she could watch people walking their dogs, riding bikes, waiting for the bus. It was leafy and green in Seattle during those months, and the window provided a beautiful panoramic movie of city life in the summer.

My father died twelve years earlier, and my mother never talked about him much. Yet suddenly with the illness, she began to talk about him many times a day. She recalled stories I'd heard many times—but she also began to share details of her forty-year-plus marriage to him which I had never heard.

She also began to see him.

She saw him first in spirit form, a misty white apparition that she noticed floating in the nursing home corridor. She was terrified at first, until she realized it was my dad.

I didn't see him; I haven't yet seen spirit in that form.

But what I did begin to experience was communication from my father and my two grandmothers, who began to show up almost daily to talk with me about my mother.

They showed me my mother and father as spirit flames together: you might call them twin flames, but there was the knowing that there were more than two flames that belong in this particular soul cluster. They appeared childlike, running hand in hand over a rolling hill, deliriously happy. They were giggling and laughing, and they looked like they could fly.

I also saw my paternal grandmother preparing a great welcome chair for my mother for whenever her time was to come. It was loaded with flowers, twinkling lights, and other delights. "This will help her not be afraid," my grandmother said.

My father was also preparing to meet my mother. He showed himself standing on one side of a short bridge, holding out his hand to her. She grasped it and walked toward him.

Finally, my maternal grandmother showed up, a bit worried. "We don't want her to be afraid," she told me. And then whisked away to take care of something.

As I write this, my mother is at home recovering from her illness. I hope she's going to get well and be fine. Yet when the veil has been lifted so clearly, we begin to understand that transition is something we will each face, in our time.

Spirits, guides, ascended masters, angels. These all seem like terms that don't make sense, until you begin to experience them for yourself. These entities are available to each of us, and in fact, they are helping us at all moments, even if we don't believe it.

In belief, there is a great healing of the heart.

A loved one's passing no longer holds the same pain. We see that they are welcomed with joy, with festivity, with the greatest homecoming on the other side.

———

Consider those spirits who are waiting to welcome each of your family members and yourself when the time for transition has arrived. This may not be for many months, years, decades. It may be sooner than we think. The mystery is the mystery. Hold this idea of Divine homecoming in your mind and allow this to open your heart.

83
Mary's song

A few years ago I attended the funeral of a friend's mother—a woman I'd never met. We drove deep into the Oregon country that Saturday morning—but not the fields and farmland you'd expect. Instead, this was rougher land, framed in mountains and heavy with fir, and as we drove farther into the forest, the air became wet with mist.

My son, then nine, had come along. He was immediately whisked through the church doors and corralled to help as go-fer to the kitchen ladies: Shirley, Molly, and Dena. These three had spent their whole lives running community events like these—casseroles into the oven, punch measured and mixed, temperature tested for the potato salad. They knew where everything was, how everything worked, when to wait, and when to rush. They smiled sweetly and did not get in each other's way. They thanked you when you brought a plate back, so you could walk back to your table and feel like you'd done a good deed.

I was put on greeter duty. I stood behind a small table, catching people's eyes they came in, asking if they'd please sign the guest book. Many brought cards, which were placed in a basket.

"Watch these cards," a relative whispered to me. "They've got cash in them."

I'd never heard of this tradition.

"Dad's not doing too well on his finances," another relative whispered to me, "This loss is gonna be tough on him."

There was not much hugging. There were seven brothers and two daughters, but a son and daughter each had been lost twenty years ago, one in an car wreck, another in a boating accident, exactly a year apart. Dad, Mary's bereaved husband, and the rest of the immediate family sat in the second row, not the front, with boxes of tissues carefully placed about every four feet. The sobbing was audible over the music.

I stayed in the entryway for a long time, helping to direct stragglers. One man arrived late and could not decide on where to write his name in the guest book. He was past seventy, blue suit tight on his shoulders, shirt wrinkled, nails overgrown. He had to stoop down and lean on the table with one hand in order to write, as many of them had.

"My writing's not so good," they apologized.

"I need my glasses to do this."

This particular man had to bend over so far that I saw the pink of his scalp, whorls of white hair combed across.

"What line do I write at?" he asked, and I put my finger on a line for him, so he could see where to start.

Charles, he wrote carefully, the letters shaking. This was on the first line.

"Where's it go?" he asked again, and I hovered my finger around in the general area. He wrote *Smythe Sr.* on the second line, then changed his mind and wrote *Smythe Sr.* again on the line above.

"That'd cover it," he said, or maybe I just thought he said this. "Where's the men's?"

Everybody brought something. There were three potato salads, two Jell-O salads, wide stainless pans overflowing with fried chicken, a platter of sliced ham, three different green salads, one small bean salad, and pies, six different kinds. Many, many packaged trays of cookies, muffins, fresh cut fruit, veggies. The food did not fit easily on the two long, eight-foot tables covered with plastic tablecloths, and when the service was done people lined up on both sides, as the kitchen staff bustled to put out more.

They ate it all. They filled their plates and sat and ate and filled their plates again. They stayed all afternoon. There was not much laughing.

But there was much talk, this was a family, you could see that clear enough, in the rounded noses, the bald heads, the barrel chests of the men. In the wide cheekbones of the women, the curling brown hair.

"We're Missourians come over," one man said, as if that explained everything. But something in the settling had changed them generations back, as they learned to live in these mountains filled with fir trees, the road steaming with mist. By the end of the afternoon, my son had met four men named Charles, all over seventy, every one stooped and balding…

The service, for Mary, my friend's mother, made me cry. Because all the tissue had been reserved for the family, I sat in the back row and wiped my cheeks with the pads of my fingers, pushing the tears away into the air, where they might evaporate like mist around me.

We sang "Amazing Grace."

"Come in on the first verse," the soloist said, a plump man with a voice like a rock star. But we all sang every verse. It was Mary's favorite song.

———

Every life is amazing. What we do and what we don't do; how we live and who we know; the families we come from and the families we create. It is not just our own kin who are deserving of celebration—it is each of us, all our lives. Give gratitude now, for the souls who have touched you in your own life.

84

Birthing into death

When a person's body begins to transition, it's a very particular process.

The breathing goes different. There may be fluids draining from the mouth and nose. They may twitch or move in ways that are disturbing. They may appear to be in a coma, or sliding in and out of states of lucidity.

At this point, they are in a state of active dying, as the hospice nurse told my brother and me a few hours before my father's passing. They are in a state of active transition.

It is scary and confusing to the people in attendance, especially if you have never seen someone pass before. It was certainly scary to me.

What if my father dies while I am in the room? What if my father dies while I am out of the room, and I'm not there to support him at this moment of passing? Can he even hear me? Does he know I'm here? What if I do something wrong? How can I even bear this pain? How can this possibly be the end?

For the person transitioning, for the person dying…they don't have these concerns.

And of course, there's nothing that be done wrong, at this point. There's nothing we can fail at, at this point. We're just there, witnessing. Holding space. Being in the mystery.

Of course, death isn't unnatural. It's around us all the time. We see it all the time: the plant withered in the bowl, the possum on the road, the bird who dove straight into the plate glass window.

What's harder is the death of those we love, with whom we have a soul connection: The dog who's been a source of comfort and companionship for many years. The cat we adored. And of course, the people in our lives.

It may be a person we've had the great joy to be with for twenty, forty, sixty years or more. We've had a long, long time with them, and yet it's still not enough. In those last moments, when they are going, we would give anything…anything…to have more time with them.

To simply be in their presence.

As if all the silly arguments and frustrations of all the years prior, and even all the deeper wounds between us simply dissolve in those last weeks, days, and hours, when we know they will be leaving.

Perhaps even sadder is the loss of those bright spirits we've just gotten to know: the child who dies too young. The love you've only just found at any age, transitioning before you had enough time.

Death takes away.

Even when the veil is thin—and the veil nowadays is very thin—we don't get the same comfort from spirit as we do from the human, living and being in front of us.

It may be in some evolution of consciousness that death no longer exists: the way Jesus spoke of eternal life. But on this planet, only a very few have achieved that level of understanding.

For most of us death means goodbye, even with spirit connection. It is unbearable. And yet this is the path we will all walk, the passage we will all enter.

My father was off all ventilators and tubes and medications by the time he was actively dying. He was alone in a dim, quiet room, a beautiful hospice room that looked out to a picture window of a beautiful garden. On the lawn, there were crows: fifteen of them, sixteen. Dressed in black, for mourning.

At the time, I didn't care about the crows, what they meant, or what they signified. All I could see were my father's hands, my father's arms, which I'd seen a million times in my life, but that suddenly looked different, as if I couldn't recognize them at all.

The essence of him, the soul presence, was already moving, gathering momentum to make the transition. His body continued to shut down: fluid poured out of my father's nose and mouth. His breathing had slowed and deepened, as if he was in the middle of the deepest dream.

Except he would not awaken again, into this reality.

My father was a brilliant man; a PhD from Harvard. A successful man, who wrote and taught and connected and traveled. And yet here, on this bed, he was just a man outside of all those earthly markers. None of that mattered any more except as experiences.

I don't know what your belief systems are; at that point of death, it seems that most any belief system might do. In the hospice room, there was a Bible. I read it to my father sheepishly, for it wasn't his religion.

I blessed him shyly, but with absolute certainly that a blessing must be done. If I had been who I am now, I would have done things with more confidence. But I was younger then, unsure. I did not want to fail.

In the end, my father waited to die when I was out of the room; sometimes this happens, the hospice nurse told us. Sometimes people choose to go alone.

In the weeks and months that followed, I frequently saw my father as spirit. Sometimes I still see him.

I was grateful to have been there to midwife him into death in the limited way I assisted. Perhaps not the whole way; perhaps not the best way. But in the only way I could do at the time.

In the waning light of the hospice room, standing at my father's bedside, experiencing him for the last time in his physical form, I knew that he was not afraid.

He could see the light, he could see the transition, and he headed toward it like a baby being birthed.

———

At some point in your life, you will have the opportunity to birth someone into death. Do not be afraid. This is a great honor, to be with someone in his or her last moments. If you have done this with someone, remember it now in gratitude. If you feel you missed something, or failed to do something, or did something wrong, let this go now, forever.

85

The container is the mystery

The breath stops. The heart stops. The transition is complete.

We birth from life into death, our consciousness continuing on as soul.

The body is cleansed. The body is swaddled. The soul emerges into a new place: into the next life, into Oneness, into where we know not.

This is the mystery, this is the container, this is the reason that we are able to look at everything with gratitude in our hearts.

Because we do not have all the time in the world. We only have our own time.

Each moment, when looked at under the magnifying glass, is perfect. Each moment, when looked at with the expansive view of the big picture, is perfect. Each moment, when expressed as deep and certain knowing, is perfect.

Even the mystery is absolutely perfect.

When someone dies, our hearts may be broken by the way we miss them. When it is our time to die, we may be heartbroken to leave those we love.

Yet this is simply how it is.

For it is within the container between birth and death that we are able to live our most full lives—with all the heartbreak, with all the learning, with all the growth, with all the love.

———

Take a moment to review all that you have learned on this gratitude journey. Look at your own container, your birth, your childhood, your adulthood, and consider the time that you have left—whether you know what this is, or if it is still a mystery. Consider again the container of your life. Consider also the miracle of this actual moment, right here, right now. Breathe in. Breathe out. The miracle is now.

86

The feast of everything

We don't know what we think about our lives until we rub shoulders with death.

Our near death moments don't always involve seeing a white light at the end of the tunnel, angels and guides welcoming us into the light. Yes, these are experiences people commonly have.

Some report seeing a movie of all the moments in their lives; everything plays out instantaneously, yet at a pace where they can understand it all perfectly.

This was my life. This is what I did. This is how I acted. This is who I loved. This is what I learned.

Rubbing shoulders with death doesn't have to mean you nearly die, either. Other shocks to the system can have a similar effect—say, the near miss of a traffic accident that shakes us up. The phone call from a doctor, informing us we have a health problem. Getting sick, and not getting better in the way we planned. Experiencing violence. Witnessing violence. Being in a war. All of these shock us—our human system of body and mind cannot deal with these easily.

My own near death experience in 2000 did not have a white tunnel or a white light, or a movie of my life fast forwarding in my head. Instead, while in it, I simply felt blessed; blessed and more blessed for all that I had experienced.

I was rich with my experiences. I was rich with who I had loved. I was rich with what I had learned.

Everything I'd ever done wrong—and there was much of this—didn't really matter any more. Everything I'd done right—the people I'd loved and helped—I was so grateful for these experiences. In those moments, in which I did not know if I would live or die, I felt above all things grateful.

I am grateful. I have been blessed. Thank you.

And in the moment of these realizations, a golden light filled everything, and I had the idea that this was God/Universe/One/All. Not angels. Not guides. Something even more.

I recognized this in my very soul.

Years later, I look upon my experience of near death as a changing point in my life. In the months and years to follow, I began my very long education of the realization that the Universe was love. When I met death, I lost my fear and anxiety about it; and in this way, I slowly began to lose the habits of irritation, frustration, anger.

I began to learn to just *be* in my life, because I understood it was a rich feast of everything. There is nothing else like it.

It is dazzling to have consciousness, and with this body and mind that we are given to have these experiences in on earth.

Even the biggest life—the most lauded, the most successful—means nothing at the end. Even the smallest life—the least ambitious, the least successful—means everything at the end.

Simply living is a miracle of the highest magnitude.

If you've ever rubbed shoulders with death, you know this already.

Life is precious. Life is precarious. It is a gift to simply be here.

———

Consider a moment when you were at risk, when you nearly died, or when you thought you might die. Close your eyes and go back to that memory. Place yourself in that experience. Look again at what you felt or understood when you were in that experience. Look again at how your life changed from that point on, and hold gratitude for what you have learned.

87
My father's gift

It's forty-eight hours before my surgery, and I'm trying to quell the rising panic. So much is unknown: Is the melanoma cleared? Am I safe? Am I whole? Will my life continue as planned? Or the other deeper, darker spiral that I try to keep from my mind: Am I sick? Has the cancer spread? And the very worst: am I dying? The fear has caught on my shoe like a burr attaches to a shoelace on an afternoon hike in the woods.

It's there, stuck fast to everything.

It's hard to pry off, this fear. It catches on the fibers of my shoelace, and when I try to pull it free the stickers are so tiny, so microscopic, they burrow into my fingers as well. I can hardly shake them off my hand, let alone my shoe.

I'd like to detach from this fear, dispose of it, but it keeps showing up again. I'll get rid of it for a while, then I look down and there it is, nagging at my heel, and I realize that this is the lesson that I am learning now: how to live without fear, regardless of outcome.

And I realize that this is also the lesson I have been circling around my entire life: my terror at learning to swim, my panic at learning to ride a bike, my anxiety at starting school, my fear of everything that is new, different, bad, good. Always the fear circling, attaching, hobbling.

I am no longer young, a girl clinging to her father's arms in the swimming pool. I am older now, and I have been through much. Even with what I have witnessed and borne, I still believe in the innate beauty and goodness of this life.

I close my eyes, and I breathe in through the nose and out of the mouth and I sink into a meditation in which the Divine will arrive and show me the way. I seek peace, comfort, an opening into a place or state in which the gratitude is so overwhelming, there is no possible room for more—until more comes, and the heart swells in further expansion, and the heart is expanded again.

I close my eyes and breathe into this space, and to my surprise instead of this transcendent state, my father arrives to me as a vision. He's been departed these past twelve years, but he shows up clearly to me, and he has something in his hands.

It's a box of Life Savers, the kind I used to give him every Christmas as a gift because he said he wanted them.

"That's all I want from you," he would tell me every year. "Nothing would make me happier."

So every year from about ages five to ten, it was the same thing: I'd save up my money, and go buy the Lifesavers. Not a single roll, but the multi pack, the special holiday gift pack.

There were all kinds of Life Savers in the gift pack: a roll of wintergreen, his favorite for the way they crunched and sparked in his mouth. Butterscotch, my favorite for the way they were creamy to the end. Rainbow, a mix of lime, lemon, pineapple, orange, and cherry, which we'd eat when our favorite flavors were gone. And root beer, which we'd avoid eating until weeks later, and finally throw in the trash.

It became our tradition after school: I'd put down my backpack and head into his office where the Life Saver gift pack would be waiting on his desk, and we'd choose our favorite flavors, and eat them—sucking or crunching as the mood of the day dictated—until they were finally gone.

Now, he's holding the box out to me.

"It's Life Savers," he says to me, and I strain toward him, trying to understand what he means.

Suddenly, a single wintergreen candy pops into my mind, all fresh and green and minty, and in a flash I understand what he is saying.

"It's a Life Saver," he says again, more insistently, pushing the box toward me, and I realize he is talking about my surgery. *The surgery is a life saver*, he says again into my mind, so loudly I cannot miss it.

My fears fall away. I'm sitting with awe pumping through my body, as once again I realize the true nature of reality:

My father, though departed, has arrived to me over the years since his passing, and his messages have been consistent and clear. Everything he has told me has been accurate. Everything he has said has come to pass.

But this message is the most clear on a day when I truly need clarity—and hope most of all. It's the symbol of his love for me, this Life Saver gift pack we held as our Christmas tradition so many years ago. It's also the clearest message.

The surgery is a life saver.

This experience will save my life, he is telling me. And on a new, deeper level that I am just beginning to understand, this experience will also save me, from living a life spent in fear.

I am learning to shake the burr off my shoe before it attaches. To step carefully onto the path where love and light and true reality reside. The path is not easy to find all the time. But this is my new lesson: to life without fear. To live in gratitude in each moment. Not as if it were the last—but as if it were the first.

———

Review your life today. What burrs are on your shoe? What fears still cling to you? What do your dearly departed have to offer you? Close your eyes and ask them. Do not be surprised when they arrive easily into your vision. The departed are always with us; the soul connections never leave us. Take a moment and experience yourself from the perspective of soul. Understand with deepest gratitude that your true reality, your true experience, is as an eternal, Divine being.

88

The moment is now

It's less than a millimeter; in fact, it's less than half a centimeter.

If you have a metric ruler you can see how small this is—impossibly small. If you do not have a metric ruler, you may imagine it this way: it is the size of the period at the end of this sentence.

This tiny micrometastis of cancer cells is just 39 millimeters, but it is the reason I will undergo a second surgery two weeks after my first one, to remove the lymph nodes under my right armpit.

"There is the option to wait and see," my surgeon tells me, laying out my choices. He's a good man, father of five, and has been nothing but smart, compassionate, and aware during this process. "That's always an option you have," he continues, "but the outcomes are not as good. And with your kids…"

With my kids. With my partner. With my work, my clients, my friends, my life. I feel my face heat up in a way it's been doing lately;

cheeks burning, the mind failing to fasten onto reality, the very real possibility that I might throw up. This new information, these new lab results, are too much to take in.

And yet…I do not have to wait and see. I can take the moment, this moment that is now, and I can do this new surgery, and it will work or it won't work, but at the very least I am acting on my own behalf, with the technology that is available to me in this day and age, and the angels as always, will surround me and keep me.

I realize I am saying all of this aloud to him, and I can't stop myself.

When I had the near death experience in 2000, I hear myself tell him, I knew in that instant where I almost died but did not die, how beautiful beyond description my life had been up until that moment: how full and rich and blessed.

I see him nod.

When I am faced with this situation now, I tell him—I want to live! I love my life! And yet the blessings I have received have been so much more than one person or soul could have even imagined— the good of it, the bad, all of it. Every moment, infinite blessing.

The moment of our deaths is unknown to us. We spend all this time thinking we'll live to be eighty-two or ninety-seven or a hundred and five, when in fact many of us will die very much younger. None of us knows for sure.

It is this moment that we are assured. This moment of now. If we're very lucky, we'll get another moment of now. If we're extraordinarily blessed, yet another.

We're souls. We're bright lights. Our journey goes on and on. But as humans, in our tender and precarious earth bodies, it is our blessing to experience these moments of now fully, in the deepest way: the good, the bad, the all of it.

I call my partner from the car in the hospital parking lot. I call my mother next.

I drive home, and turn on the heat and as the house warms I sit on the sofa wrapped in a big blanket and I cry and cry and cry. I can't stop crying. Then I cry some more. The tears pour down my face as I list all the reasons to God that I simply can't die.

While at the same moment realizing that I can die, and some-day—sooner or later—I will. And this is my path, and this is the journey of every soul. Birth to death.

And then I realize the crying is making my voice rough, and I need to do my radio show at 4 p.m. that afternoon. And I climb out of the blanket and head into my office, where I prepare my notes for the show. I'll broadcast live to thousands of listeners, and hundreds of thousands more on digital streaming.

That's a lot of souls to connect with ...

At 3:55 pm I enter a new moment. I slip on my headphones, check my computer systems, organize my notes once again, close my eyes, and head into prayer, and the feed comes in from my producer, and I am live on air.

I don't remember any of the next hour. I'm talking, I'm laughing, I'm watching my screen, and I take call after call from people all over the U.S.: Sandi from Ohio, Marika from Seattle, Evelyn from California, more souls and more souls. I have no idea what I say, but the imagery and information comes quickly to me, and I recognize that I am laughing and my producer is laughing and the energy in the room is buzzing with light and I'm so blissed out with the energy of the show that I practically levitate out of my chair when the time slot is done.

I'm burning with adrenaline, I'm in this now moment, and I throw on my coat and head outside, and walk round the circular driveway loop forty times by the time my partner arrives home from work. The leaves are stacked a foot high on the ground, and it's raining, and he gets out of his car and joins me, and we walk around the circle until it's too dark to see farther, the leaves whirling down, the winter geese crying above, and we are talking, crying, laughing, walking in this mystic night, our hearts blazing open in this moment that is now.

It's all we are given: this moment. It's all we are given: this now.

When we are truly living, our hearts blaze open and they keep opening through everything that arrives to us in each new now: the good, the bad, the all of it. Life's always more than you can handle, when you're truly in the now. It's always more than you could ever imagine, this blessing that is the reality of your life.

———

If you are ready to live in gratitude—not for the past, not for the future, but for the moment, your heart blazing open and then opening again—then begin this now. If you want to really live your life, there is no other way but to live it in wonder and awe and thanks.

Part Twelve:
Birth

....

*In which we emerge yet again,
a new soul in the world.*

Epilogue:
There is only one entrance

The soul is fully aware as it begins its transition. It's conscious, it's cognizant—and most of all, it's excited! It's brimming with plans—places to go, people to see in this new lifetime it's about to enter. It can't wait to get some more soul lessons under its belt, to revisit with those souls it already knows so well—to take that grand ride together once again. It can't wait to get started on its to-do list for this next lifetime.

Bursting with excitement, the soul straps on its landing gear and starts the treacherous path to inhabiting a body. It's tiny for a while, its whole world nothing more than heartbeat and warm fluid. Then it gets bigger, and space gets more crowded, and muffled sounds come in from somewhere, and it turns and kicks in excitement to get out, get started!

But the soul, eager as it is, is still prudent. It uses its last months in the womb to review what it has learned in the past lifetime: the soul lessons it learned, the soul lessons it failed to learn, the people it needs to fix karma with, the people from whom it needs to learn. It's so exciting, the soul knows, to have all this knowledge, and to burst forth into the world with all this remembrance, and to finally make it right this lifetime!

One day, the soul realizes that birth is imminent. Its body has flipped upside down, its head being pulled toward gravity. There is contracting and pushing and bearing down. There is the long descent down a dark tunnel, a heading toward the white light. The soul takes one last minute to collect its thoughts to ensure remembering everything upon emergence, and then suddenly, unexpectedly, there is a great final push and the soul is out into the white light, born of a human body, a baby covered in blood and mucus, being swaddled and held to its mother.

The baby lets out its first cry. Not because it is too cold, or because the light too glaring after all those months of darkness, as we have been led to believe.

No, the baby lets out its first cry because it realizes that it has forgotten everything it ever knew. It's all been left behind—the soul lessons, the destiny, the grand plans, the karma, the consciousness, the awareness, the understanding that all is One/All/Divine/Universe/Love—it's all been forgotten in this momentous transition from untethered soul to soul incarnate, in the act of birthing into this world, as it is with every baby being birthed into the world.

The soul must learn it all again.

Comforted by mother, father, beings it cannot yet remember, the soul once again begins its journey of experiencing life as Divine being in earth body.

It will take an entire lifetime to remember what it has forgotten.

It will take an entire lifetime to learn what it already knows.

And thus, the journey of soul growth continues.

Bibliography

Brach, Tara. *Radical Acceptance: Embracing Your Life with the Heart of a Buddha*. New York: Bantam, 2004.

Burkeman, Oliver. *The Antidote: Happiness for People Who Can't Stand Positive Thinking*. New York: Faber and Faber, 2012.

Chodron, Pema. *When Things Fall Apart: Heart Advice for Difficult Times*. Boston: Shambhala, 2000.

Chopra, Deepak. *The Book of Secrets: Unlocking the Hidden Dimensions of Your Life*. New York: Three Rivers Press, 2004.

Dass, Ram, and Paul Gorman. *How Can I Help? Stories and Reflections on Service*. New York: Random House, 1985.

Gick, Bryan, and Donald Derrick. "Aero-tactile Integration in Speech Perception." *Nature* 462 (2008): 502–504.

Graer, Victor A. "Some Notable Features of Pygmy and Bushmen Polyphonic Practice, With Special Reference to Survivals of Traditional Vocal Polyphony in Europe," The Proceedings of the Fourth International Symposium on Traditional Polyphony, 2008, via http://www.polyphony.ge/uploads/fortheng/09_grauer_eng.pdf.

Kornfield, Jack. *The Buddha Is Still Teaching*. Boston: Shambala, 2011.

McCraty, Rollin, et al. "The Electricity of Touch: Detection and Measurement of Cardiac Energy Exchange Between People," *Brain and Values: Is a Biological Science of Values Possible?* (1998): 359–379, via: http://www.heartmath.org/research/research-publications/electricity-of-touch.html.

Rubin, Gretchen. *The Happiness Project*. New York: HarperCollins, 2009.

Schmidt, Amy. *Knee Deep in Grace: The Extraordinary Life and Teaching of Dipa Ma*. Lajunaluska, NC: Present Perfect Book, 2013.

Tompkins, Peter, and Christopher Bird. *The Secret Life of Plants*. New York: HarperCollins, 1973.

"Platypus Genome Explains Animal's Peculiar Features; Holds Clues to Evolution of Mammals." May 2008. Washington University School of Medicine, via *ScienceDaily*: http://www.sciencedaily.com/releases/2008/05/080507131453.htm.

Weil, Andrew. *Spontaneous Happiness*. New York: Little, Brown & Company, 2011.

Wiseman, Sara. *Becoming Your Best Self: The Guide to Clarity, Inspiration and Joy*. Woodbury, MN: Llewellyn, 2012.

_____. *The Four Passages of the Heart: Moving from Pain into Love*. Bedford, IN: Norlights, 2012.

Your Psychic Child
How to Raise Intuitive & Spiritually Gifted Kids of All Ages
Sara Wiseman

Want to take an active role in your child's psychic and spiritual development? This indispensable guide helps parents understand and nurture their uniquely gifted children.

Learn about the psychic awakening process and the talents that emerge with each age, from toddler to teen. Discover how to gently encourage your children to explore and develop their strengths in clairvoyance, energy healing, or mediumship. Teach him or her how to connect with the Divine. Anchored in down-to-earth parental wisdom and alive with personal anecdotes, *Your Psychic Child* is an essential resource for parents who recognize their child's psychic and spiritual potential.

978-0-7387-2061-6, 312 pp., 6 x 9   **$17.95**

108 Practices to Live a
Divinely Inspired Life

Awake
in the
world

DEBRA MOFFITT

Awake in the World
108 Practices to Live a Divinely Inspired Life
Debra Moffitt

Everyone needs an anchor in this fast-paced and chaotic world. *Awake in the World* offers 108 easy ways to weave soul-nourishing peace and divinity into each day.

This engaging and practical guide was inspired by the author's own personal quest for spiritual enrichment. The practices she brought back from a journey around the world changed her life—and can transform yours. Drawn from an array of wisdom traditions, these 108 bite-sized exercises—involving meditation, labyrinth walking, inspired lovemaking, mantras, and ritual—are quick and simple to do. By sharpening your spiritual awareness, you'll learn to cultivate calm in a crisis, focus on what is truly important, and recognize the divine in everyday life. To support and encourage you on this exciting journey of self-discovery, the author shares her own personal, moving stories.

978-0-7387-2722-6, 432 pp., 5 x 7   **$16.95**

Melissa Alvarez

365 Ways

*

to RAISE Your

*

FREQUENCY

SIMPLE TOOLS TO INCREASE
YOUR SPIRITUAL ENERGY
FOR BALANCE, PURPOSE, AND JOY

365 Ways to Raise Your Frequency
Simple Tools to Increase Your Spiritual Energy for Balance, Purpose, and Joy
Melissa Alvarez

The soul's vibrational rate, our spiritual frequency, has a huge impact on our lives. As it increases, so does our capacity to calm the mind, connect with angels and spirit guides, find joy and enlightenment, and achieve what we want in life.

This simple and inspiring guide makes it easy to elevate your spiritual frequency every day. Choose from a variety of ordinary activities, such as singing and cooking. Practice visualization exercises and techniques for reducing negativity, manifesting abundance, tapping into Universal Energy, and connecting with your higher self. Discover how generous actions and a positive attitude can make a difference. You'll also find long-term projects and guidance for boosting your spiritual energy to new heights over a lifetime.

978-0-7387-2740-0, 432 pp., 5 x 7   **$16.95**

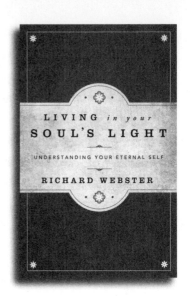

LIVING *in your*
SOUL'S LIGHT

UNDERSTANDING YOUR ETERNAL SELF

RICHARD WEBSTER

Living in Your Soul's Light
Understanding Your Eternal Self
RICHARD WEBSTER

In 2010, popular author Richard Webster had a brush with death that compelled him to write this book on the soul, the spiritual and immortal part of each of us.

Friendly and accessible, this guide explores beliefs and customs regarding the soul, past lives, and reincarnation in cultures all over the world. Richard explains auras, chakras, and soul mates. He discusses the Seven Rays, powerful universal energies that have a profound effect on the soul. Richard reveals how each of the Seven Rays is related to a specific life purpose, and presents quizzes, meditations, and exercises designed to help readers determine their ray and soul purpose for this lifetime.

978-0-7387-3249-7, 264 pp., 5³⁄₁₆ x 8   **$15.95**

DON'T GIVE UP
UNTIL YOU DO

From Mindfulness to Realization
on the Buddhist Path

FRED H. MEYER, MD

Don't Give Up Until You Do
From Mindfulness to Realization on the Buddhist Path
FRED H. MEYER, MD

Walk the path of the Buddhist and reach the pinnacle of human achievement—the realization of Truth.

With warmth and simplicity, *Don't Give Up Until You Do* introduces this experience-based discipline in which the path itself is the goal. Dr. Fred Meyer, a practicing Buddhist for over thirty-five years, shares his wholehearted approach to attaining realization and offers guidance on central Buddhist concepts—from the spiritual power of humor to the dangers of possessive love to the challenge of releasing attachment. Stories of enlightenment further illustrate the importance of cultivating resolve, meditation as a means for shedding the ego, serenity of the natural world, and the true nature of reality.

Filled with practical Buddhist wisdom, this book shows that we can all attain realization by approaching the path with a pure heart and total trust.

978-0-7387-3284-8, 264 pp., 5³⁄₁₆ x 8 **$15.95**
